ACTS

MARK DRISCOLL

ACTS

STUDY GUIDE   CHAPTERS 1-5

Visit Resurgence Publishing online at www.theresurgence.com.

Resurgence Publishing, LLC, the Resurgence "R," and Resurgence wordmark are registered trademarks of Resurgence.

Acts Study Guide

Cover design: Mars Hill Creative

ISBN-10: 1938805143
ISBN-13: 978-1-938805-14-1

Printed in the United States of America

19   18   17   16   15   14   13
7   6   5   4   3   2   1

CONTENTS

INTRODUCTION

"But you will receive power when the Holy Spirit has come upon you, and you will be my witnesses in Jerusalem and in all Judea and Samaria, and to the end of the earth."

—JESUS (ACTS 1:8)

CHRISTIANITY BEGAN UNDER heavy spiritual fire, and the book of Acts is a retelling of the war. A scholar studies war history because it's an interesting subject. A soldier studies war history because he wants to win battles.

The book of Acts recounts the amazing events that occurred as the news of Jesus' life, death, and resurrection spread throughout the ancient world. Mass conversions, spontaneous baptisms, miraculous deeds, sacrificial giving, and bold evangelism took place in the face of intense persecution that included riots, beatings, and imprisonment at the hands of the religious establishment and the Roman government.

Unfortunately, many contemporary Christians approach the book of Acts like scholars instead of soldiers, as if the content were merely a record of what God did once upon a time. But the same Holy Spirit who empowered the early church remains with the church today. The incredible things we read about in the book of Acts can and should still be happening, because the Holy Spirit is the one responsible for the astounding acts you are about to study, and he is as alive, well, and active as ever. The book of Acts is one thorough illustration of what it means to live as the church on mission for Jesus, empowered by his guiding grace and supernatural presence.

The early church movement grew in the face of adversity because the first believers lived by the power of the Holy Spirit. Not only that, they fully expected to live as

Jesus had—hated, betrayed, and assaulted, but always rejoicing because their hope and joy did not come from this world. That's what it means to live as a Christian.

This study is theologically robust and is meant to be much more than an academic analysis of the biblical text. Whether you choose to work through the Daily Devotions, the Small Group Study, the Group Inductive Study, or all three, I hope this book helps you develop regular rhythms of Bible study that make sense for you, your family, and your community.

As you study, I pray that God compels you to live courageously on mission. The book of Acts teaches us that the Holy Spirit shows up in power when the church lives on mission for Jesus.

—*Pastor Mark Driscoll*

COMPONENTS OF THIS STUDY GUIDE

This study guide is the result of a collaborative effort between Pastor Mark Driscoll and Mars Hill Church staff, Docent Research Group, and faithful volunteers. This eleven-week study comprises three parts:

1. Daily Devotions
2. Small Group Study
3. Group Inductive Study

The **Daily Devotions** were written to facilitate dinnertime conversation with your family. These reflections are geared toward a younger audience but are written in a way that will be challenging to all. Five devotions are provided for each week's Scripture passage, and you're encouraged to use these in whatever way best fits the weekly rhythms of your family.

The **Small Group Study** is intended for small group Bible studies. Many churches encourage these types of midweek studies, and each shares the same goal—that the people of God gather together in community to study the Word, encourage one another, pray, and get equipped for the mission of making the gospel of Jesus known to each group member, their families and communities.

The **Group Inductive Study** encourages digging deep into Scripture and employs an in-depth reading technique set in a discussion-based setting. An inductive study asks the questions, "What does the Bible say, and what does it mean?" "What do we observe, and how should we interpret it in light of the whole truth of the Bible?" This portion of the study guide focuses on delving deep into the text in a collaborative environment and is a great complement to the Daily Devotions and Small Group Study material.

For additional resources on how to use these studies, please refer to the Appendix for Leaders.

DAILY DEVOTIONS

WEEK 1

Acts 1:1–11

DAY 1

The resurrection of Jesus by the power of the Spirit

> [1:3] He presented himself alive to them after his suffering by many proofs, appearing to them during forty days and speaking about the kingdom of God. [4] And while staying with them he ordered them not to depart from Jerusalem, but to wait for the promise of the Father, which, he said, "you heard from me; [5] for John baptized with water, but you will be baptized with the Holy Spirit not many days from now."

Have you ever been to a party and observed a guest who was just bursting with energy, happiness, and joy?

The person couldn't stop laughing, telling jokes, and having a good time. Oftentimes someone will say, "I want what he's got"—meaning, "I wish I could be as joy-filled as that guy."

Do you ever read the accounts of Jesus in the Gospels and think, *I want what he's got!*? Do you ever wish you could heal people or speak with authority or pray as he did? The Bible says that Jesus was filled with the Holy Spirit (Luke 1:15; 4:1). The power that Jesus had was from the Spirit of God in him.

Isn't it amazing that the text for today says that, as believers in Jesus, we are filled (i.e., "baptized") with that same power? In some ways, the whole book of Acts is about how those who follow Jesus, when they are filled with God's Spirit and follow his lead, can do amazing things that give glory to God and build his church.

The truth is, if you have trusted in Jesus for salvation by giving your life to him, you *do* have what he's got.

Read *Luke 11:11–13*

- Do you love to get presents from your friends or family?
- Did you know God is a loving Father who enjoys giving good gifts?
- All parents love to see their children's faces light up on Christmas morning or birthdays when presents are unwrapped. In the same way, God loves to

give his Spirit to his children. The same power that raised Jesus from the dead is available to those who come to him as Savior and Lord, confessing their need and repenting of their sin. All you need to do is ask, and God will fill you with his Spirit, giving you new desires to serve and follow him, along with power to live a life that glorifies him through word and deed.

Prayer

Ask God to give you more of his Spirit. He loves to do it when we ask.

DAY 2

The kingdom of God—part 1

[1:6] So when they had come together, they asked him, "Lord, will you at this time restore the kingdom to Israel?" [7] He said to them, "It is not for you to know times or seasons that the Father has fixed by his own authority. [8] But you will receive power when the Holy Spirit has come upon you, and you will be my witnesses in Jerusalem and in all Judea and Samaria, and to the end of the earth."

What is the first thing you think of when you hear the word *kingdom*? Castles? Crowns? Knights in shining armor?

Living under the rule of the powerful, oppressive Romans, Jesus' disciples naturally thought of power. They waited eagerly for the Messiah to come and do many amazing things, including helping them reclaim their land as God had promised.

So when the disciples asked Jesus if the time had arrived for him to "restore the kingdom to Israel," they were thinking more about kicking out the Romans and less about what Jesus had in mind.

What, in fact, did Jesus have in mind?

Read John 18:36

- Why did Jesus say that his kingdom is "not of this world"?
- Jesus' kingdom is not about swords, guns, or huge armies that fight epic battles. It prevails simply wherever Jesus is ruling and reigning in the hearts of his people. That is true power. That is the kingdom of God.

Prayer

Read the Lord's Prayer out loud together (Matthew 6:9–13), highlighting the portion that says, "Your kingdom come, your will be done."

DAY 3

The kingdom of God—part 2

[1:6] So when they had come together, they asked him, "Lord, will you at this time restore the kingdom to Israel?" [7] He said to them, "It is not for you to know times or seasons that the Father has fixed by his own authority. [8] But you will receive power when the Holy Spirit has come upon you, and you will be my witnesses in Jerusalem and in all Judea and Samaria, and to the end of the earth."

Have you ever been in a situation where it felt like you weren't not being included?

It didn't feel very good, did it? Imagine overhearing some of your friends talking about a huge birthday party they've been invited to attend, with plans for an amazing band, the best food from the town's top chef, and a swimming pool big enough for five hundred people. The word is being spread all around school, and everyone is talking about it.

Except you. No one came running up to you with all the details about this party. No one invited you.

Aren't you glad God is *not* like this?

God has plans for a *huge* party. There will be amazing food, great music, friends to hang out with . . . and best of all, Jesus will be there. And here is the thing: everyone is invited. But it's our job to spread the word.

We see this in today's Bible passage where it says that Jesus' followers are to be "witnesses in Jerusalem and in all Judea and Samaria, and to the end of the earth." That simply means that God wants his people (i.e., witnesses) to spread the news about his salvation to the whole world! Every single person in the world. No one is excluded.

Read Matthew 28:19–20

- Where does Jesus want us to take his message? (To the whole world, all nations.)

- Does the kingdom of God exclude anyone? (No. Disciples are to be made of all nations.)
- As we spread his message to the whole world, are we alone? (Jesus said, "I am with you always.")

Prayer

God, thank you that you are the Father of all people who come to you repenting of their sins and desiring to follow you. Please help us see others as you see them. Please help us remember that you are the God of the *whole* world. Help us have a vision for reaching the nations, especially those in which there is no church and no one to tell them about Jesus.

DAY 4

The ascension of Jesus

[1:1] In the first book, O Theophilus, I have dealt with all that Jesus began to do and teach, [2] until the day when he was taken up, after he had given commands through the Holy Spirit to the apostles whom he had chosen.

[9] And when he had said these things, as they were looking on, he was lifted up, and a cloud took him out of their sight.

Where do powerful people live? Castles? Mansions? The White House? Palaces?

For most powerful people, where they live is symbolic of their rule and indicative of how important they are. The president of the United States lives in the District of Columbia, in a huge home called the White House. The king of Morocco resides in a huge palace as a symbol of his rule over the nation. Powerful people live such locations.

The most powerful person of all, Jesus, lives in one, too. But his is much more grand than the residences of the president of the U.S. and the king of Morocco; Jesus lives in heaven and rules over *all*.

This text reminds us that when Jesus left the earth, he was "lifted up" to heaven, where he is now seated at God's right hand (Luke 22:69; Ephesians 1:20). Jesus doesn't need to live in a specific location here on earth to be powerful. His house is with God in heaven, and from there rules over all. He will stay there until the day of his return, when he sets up a new and glorious physical kingdom on earth.

Read Matthew 28:18

- Who is the most powerful person in the universe? (Jesus, who has all authority.)
- Where does he live? (Heaven, until he returns to set up heaven here on earth—Revelation 21:1–5.)

Prayer

Father, thank you for sending your Son, Jesus. We long for his return. Thank you that, as we wait, we can know you are ruling and reigning even now from heaven. We trust you and can't wait to see you again.

DAY 5

The return of Jesus

[1:10] And while they were gazing into heaven as he went, behold, two men stood by them in white robes, [11] and said, "Men of Galilee, why do you stand looking into heaven? This Jesus, who was taken up from you into heaven, will come in the same way as you saw him go into heaven."

Have you ever been separated from someone or something you love?

Maybe your parents went on vacation, or someone in your family died. Perhaps you lost a pet or a favorite possession, or a good friend moved to a different city. Everyone knows what it feels like to miss someone, to long or yearn for something. *Will I get it back? Will I see them again?*

We Christians feel this way about Jesus. He is our Savior, the one who rescues us from our sin, the world, and the devil. He laid down his life, so we could live. He is now in heaven, and we worship him in Spirit and truth as we patiently wait for the day when he returns in his physical body.

As fully God and fully man, Jesus will always and forever have a body like ours. (This shows us that God loves the physical creation he made. He himself is part of it!) With it he left the earth, and with it he will return again. And at that time, he'll give us perfect bodies that live forever, too. Never again will we be physically separated from our Lord and Savior Jesus.

DAILY DEVOTIONS

Read *Acts 3:19–21*

- Where is Jesus right now?
- What will Jesus do when he returns?
- What should we do to get ready for Jesus' return?

Prayer

Father, we long for the return of Jesus. Thank you that we don't need to fear your final judgment when you come because Jesus paid for our sins on the cross. May we be quick to repent of our sins and trust in your forgiveness. Thank you that you promise to return and make all things right.

WEEK 2

Acts 1:12–26

DAY 1

Unity in prayer

[1:12] Then they returned to Jerusalem from the mount called Olivet, which is near Jerusalem, a Sabbath day's journey away. [13] And when they had entered, they went up to the upper room, where they were staying, Peter and John and James and Andrew, Philip and Thomas, Bartholomew and Matthew, James the son of Alphaeus and Simon the Zealot and Judas the son of James. [14] All these with one accord were devoting themselves to prayer, together with the women and Mary the mother of Jesus, and his brothers.

Have you ever played sports or participated in activities with a group of people who shared a goal?

Teamwork brings a certain sense of enjoyment, fulfillment, and satisfaction. It's good to be on a team, isn't it? God created us to enjoy relationships with others who have a common vision in mind—like winning, achieving, or earning rewards.

But today's text demonstrates a goal that's even more important. In it we see believers gathering to pray. They share a common goal of surrendering their wills and actions to God and submitting themselves to him—a real prayer team!

There is no greater unity than unity that is formed by God. When we come to God together in prayer, there is great power and deep enjoyment. If you are reading this right now with your family, know that together you form a team. As a family, wouldn't it be cool to be like the first followers of Jesus, devoting yourselves to prayer as they did?

Read *Philippians 4:6–7*

- What does God want us to pray about?
- What things can we be thankful to God for?
- What happens when we pray and are thankful?

Prayer

Our Father, make us people of prayer like your first followers. May we be humble enough to admit that we don't have all the answers and need help, and may we also be humble enough to acknowledge that there is much to be thankful for. Amen.

DAY 2

The fulfillment of prophecy

[1:15] In those days Peter stood up among the brothers (the company of persons was in all about 120) and said, [16] "Brothers, the Scripture had to be fulfilled, which the Holy Spirit spoke beforehand by the mouth of David concerning Judas, who became a guide to those who arrested Jesus. [17] For he was numbered among us and was allotted his share in this ministry." [18] (Now this man acquired a field with the reward of his wickedness, and falling headlong he burst open in the middle and all his bowels gushed out. [19] And it became known to all the inhabitants of Jerusalem, so that the field was called in their own language Akeldama, that is, Field of Blood.) [20] "For it is written in the Book of Psalms,

"'May his camp become desolate,
    and let there be no one to dwell in it'; and
"'Let another take his office.'"

The Bible is divided into two main parts, the Old Testament and the New Testament. One great way to think about the differences between them is to remember that in the Old Testament, God makes many promises about what he will do in the future, and in the New Testament, he fulfills many of those promises in the life, death, and resurrection of Jesus.

Some of these Old Testament promises are called prophecies. In the Old Testament, prophecies are statements that come true at a later point in time. One Old Testament prophecy, Psalm 109:6, foretells someone betraying Jesus. This betrayer will eventually die and his role in the group given to a new person.

Jesus' first followers loved all of God's Word and took it very seriously. They knew the Old Testament very well and realized that what it predicted would come to pass. This is why, in today's text, we see the apostles replacing Judas with a new person. God said it should happen, and they are ensuring its fulfillment.

Read 2 Peter 1:21

- Where do prophecies come from—man or God?

Prayer

Our Father, may we take all of your Word seriously—just as seriously as did Jesus' first followers, whom we read about in this text. May we love your Word and long to read it, so that we can be people who are encouraged by hope. Thank you that you have spoken to us through your Word. Amen.

DAY 3

Judas had no true love for Jesus

[1:15] In those days Peter stood up among the brothers (the company of persons was in all about 120) and said, [16] "Brothers, the Scripture had to be fulfilled, which the Holy Spirit spoke beforehand by the mouth of David concerning Judas, who became a guide to those who arrested Jesus. [17] For he was numbered among us and was allotted his share in this ministry." [18] (Now this man acquired a field with the reward of his wickedness, and falling headlong he burst open in the middle and all his bowels gushed out. [19] And it became known to all the inhabitants of Jerusalem, so that the field was called in their own language Akeldama, that is, Field of Blood.) [20] "For it is written in the Book of Psalms,

"'May his camp become desolate,
     and let there be no one to dwell in it'; and
"'Let another take his office.'"

Imagine having a very close friend with whom you spend every waking hour sharing meals, games, laughter, and sorrow. Together you travel to exciting places, and your Facebook page is full of pictures of the two of you creating many cherished memories.

Now imagine that one day your friend decides he doesn't like you anymore and joins a new group of friends, who are into completely different things. Soon you find out he never really liked you at all; in fact, he was using you. He didn't love you as a person; he just loved your amazing house and the fun technology you owned.

Such is something like what happened to Jesus in his relationship with Judas,

21

who spent a lot of time in Jesus' inner circle but had no true love for him. Judas probably said many nice things to Jesus, but when push came to shove, he was willing to betray Jesus for money. How sad that Judas loved money more than Jesus.

Read *Matthew 15:7–9*

- What does it mean to be a hypocrite? (Being someone who says one thing but does another.)
- Does God just want us to say correct things about him? What more could he want from us?
- The truth is, at one time or another, all of us have been like Judas and the religious leaders of his time. We liked what Jesus could do for us more than him as a person. When have you loved gifts more than the Giver?

Prayer

Our Father, we repent of loving stuff more than you. We repent of seeing you as a way of getting what our hearts really want. May you be our greatest treasure. Increase our faith and help our unbelief. Keep us from loving the gifts you give more than loving you. Protect us from the things that lured Judas away from you. Amen.

DAY 4

Submitted decision making

[1:21] So one of the men who have accompanied us during all the time that the Lord Jesus went in and out among us, [22] beginning from the baptism of John until the day when he was taken up from us—one of these men must become with us a witness to his resurrection." [23] And they put forward two, Joseph called Barsabbas, who was also called Justus, and Matthias. [24] And they prayed and said, "You, Lord, who know the hearts of all, show which one of these two you have chosen [25] to take the place in this ministry and apostleship from which Judas turned aside to go to his own place." [26] And they cast lots for them, and the lot fell on Matthias, and he was numbered with the eleven apostles.

"Don't tell me what to do!" "You're not my boss!" "I know what to do, and I don't need you to tell me!"

Sound familiar? When we utter these types of phrases, it shows we want to be in charge. Do you ever feel like you want to be the boss?

In our text for today, we see a different example. The disciples had a very important decision to make: choosing a new person to replace Judas—someone who would be a key player in spreading the gospel.

Do you notice what they did before making this huge decision? Verse 24 says they prayed. They weren't acting bossy, were they? They knew God was Boss, and they wanted to seek his will in this momentous matter.

Read *Luke 6:12–13*

- What did Jesus do before he chose his twelve disciples?
- Do you think this was a big decision? Why?
- How is it similar to what we see the disciples doing in today's text?
- What are some things you would like to pray about?

Prayer
Lead your family in sharing prayer requests and praying about the needs mentioned.

DAY 5

Moving forward by faith

[1:21] So one of the men who have accompanied us during all the time that the Lord Jesus went in and out among us, [22] beginning from the baptism of John until the day when he was taken up from us—one of these men must become with us a witness to his resurrection." [23] And they put forward two, Joseph called Barsabbas, who was also called Justus, and Matthias. [24] And they prayed and said, "You, Lord, who know the hearts of all, show which one of these two you have chosen [25] to take the place in this ministry and apostleship from which Judas turned aside to go to his own place." [26] And they cast lots for them, and the lot fell on Matthias, and he was numbered with the eleven apostles.

Have you ever drawn straws? (Perhaps grab some straws and cut one to demonstrate how the process works.)

Sometimes people do this to choose one individual from a group for a special—or

23

not-so-special—task. Maybe you could draw straws tomorrow to determine who gets to do one special chore around the house!

In today's text, we see the disciples doing something similar. It says they "casted lots" to make the decision about who should take Judas' place. This practice for making decisions was very common in the Old Testament. Marked stones were placed in a jar and then shaken out. If your stone came out first, it meant you had been chosen.

Notice that first the disciples prayed, then they acted. They knew that God was helping them make the decision. Do you know what the word *sovereignty* means? When we say that God is sovereign, we mean that he is in complete control. The disciples believed that God was in control of whatever stone came out of the jar and believed by faith that those results indicated the choice they should make.

Read *Proverbs 16:33*

• Who ultimately decides what will come to pass?

Prayer

Our Father, help us know that you love us and that you are in control. Thank you that we can trust you because you are sovereign. May our lives honor you through the decisions we make. Amen.

WEEK 3

Acts 2:1–13

DAY 1

The sound of God, the power of God

> [2:1] When the day of Pentecost arrived, they were all together in one place. [2] And suddenly there came from heaven a sound like a mighty rushing wind, and it filled the entire house where they were sitting. [3] And divided tongues as of fire appeared to them and rested on each one of them. [4] And they were all filled with the Holy Spirit and began to speak in other tongues as the Spirit gave them utterance.

Have you ever been in a storm and felt the power of the wind blowing against your body? At times it's even impossible to stand up straight! And when the wind blows really hard, it makes a sound so loud that it is said to be "howling."

The Bible, especially the Old Testament, records that when God came to his people, they often heard what sounded like a storm or a strong wind, or they might have seen fire. So when these first believers heard a sound "like a mighty rushing wind," it doesn't necessarily mean they were in the midst of a huge windstorm; rather, what they heard could be compared to the sound a powerful wind makes. Luke, the author of Acts, couldn't find any better words to describe what he experienced.

But the point is clear: God the Holy Spirit was in their midst. And he wasn't with them just to be observed; he was there to fill them with his power.

Read *Romans 14:17*

- What will be produced when we have the Holy Spirit in our lives? (Joy.)
- What other things does God love to see in the lives of his followers? (Righteousness and peace.)

Prayer

Our Father, you have promised to give the Holy Spirit to those who ask. We ask now for more of your Holy Spirit to cause us to be thankful for everything you have done for us. May we be so thankful that we want to sing! Amen.

DAY 2

A new language for mission

[2:1] When the day of Pentecost arrived, they were all together in one place. [2] And suddenly there came from heaven a sound like a mighty rushing wind, and it filled the entire house where they were sitting. [3] And divided tongues as of fire appeared to them and rested on each one of them. [4] And they were all filled with the Holy Spirit and began to speak in other tongues as the Spirit gave them utterance. [5] Now there were dwelling in Jerusalem Jews, devout men from every nation under heaven. [6] And at this sound the multitude came together, and they were bewildered, because each one was hearing them speak in his own language.

Can you speak a language other than English? Do you know any words in Spanish or French? How about Swahili or Chinese? If you know another language, you can communicate with people from a different country and culture.

Do you know why we have different languages today? The answer is found in a story that took place a long time ago. We read about it in Genesis chapter 11. In short, a bunch of people wanted to build a huge tower to make it clear how great they were. But God didn't want them bragging about their accomplishments; instead, he wanted them bragging about *his* greatness. So can you guess what happened next?

A lot of babbling! God frustrated their plans and caused these tower builders to speak different languages. The Bible says that before this, everyone spoke the same language. Suddenly, it was quite hard for everyone to work together. Can you imagine the difficulties involved with building a huge tower when the person working next to you speaks Spanish and you don't?

God confused their speech so they wouldn't continue to be selfish and proud by building a huge tower. After this, the Bible says that people scattered over the face of the earth, resulting in the many different languages we have today.

But did you notice what happened in the text we read today? When God's people were filled with the Spirit, they were enabled to speak different languages they couldn't speak before. Why? If you remember, we learned in the first chapter of Acts that God wants us to tell every single person in the world about him. Remember verse 8, which says Christians are called to witness about Jesus "to the end of the earth"?

Enabling people to speak different languages and reach those in faraway lands was God's way of sending his people on mission to the whole world. God, in his goodness, reversed the confused speech poured out on those who started building that huge tower so long before!

Read Mark 16:15

- Where does God want us to take his news about Jesus? (To all of creation.)

Prayer

Our Father, thank you for promising to empower us when we take your message of salvation to all of creation. May you draw people to yourself from every tribe, tongue, and nation. We want to align ourselves with your mission. Give us a greater hunger for you and your glory, so that we naturally have a passion to tell people the good news of Jesus.

DAY 3

The mighty works of God

[2:7] And they were amazed and astonished, saying, "Are not all these who are speaking Galileans? [8] And how is it that we hear, each of us in his own native language? [9] Parthians and Medes and Elamites and residents of Mesopotamia, Judea and Cappadocia, Pontus and Asia, [10] Phrygia and Pamphylia, Egypt and the parts of Libya belonging to Cyrene, and visitors from Rome, [11] both Jews and proselytes, Cretans and Arabians—we hear them telling in our own tongues the mighty works of God."

Isn't it fun telling someone a really cool story about an event that completely amazed you?

Maybe you received a new video game and couldn't wait to tell your friends about it. "You won't believe these graphics!" Or maybe you saw an amazing sports play in which an athlete impressed you with her athletic skill. When you see something like that, you can hardly contain yourself, right? You're compelled to find someone and ask excitedly, "Did you see that?!"

We should feel the same way about God—so amazed at his creation and acts throughout history that we can hardly contain ourselves.

We see an example of such excitement in today's text. It says the first followers of Jesus were filled with the Holy Spirit. And what else? Did they just talk about the weather or the great meal they ate last night? No. Verse 11 of chapter 2 says they were given power to speak different languages so that they might proclaim "the mighty works of God" to people in different nations and cultures.

God's mightiest work was raising Jesus from the dead to secure our salvation. But shouldn't we also stand in awe of an amazing sunset, an eagle gracefully flying through the sky, and the radiant colors of a wildflower? Evidence of God's mighty works is around us all the time. Let's give God glory by talking to others about what he has done. He loves it when we do.

Read *Psalm 147:1–11*

- What are some reasons the psalmist gives for why we should praise God?
- What "mighty works" has he done in your life?

Prayer

God, give us eyes to see the amazing works you have done. May we stand in awe of the Cross and the Empty Tomb. And may we not be so hurried and distracted that we don't take time to experience your mighty works in creation and give you praise and adoration for that which we see. Amen.

DAY 4

There will always be opposition

[2:11] "We hear them telling in our own tongues the mighty works of God." [12] And all were amazed and perplexed, saying to one another, "What does this mean?" [13] But others mocking said, "They are filled with new wine."

It's likely you're familiar with the sports phrase "the opposing team." If you're on a soccer team, you're trying to score goals, right? But the opposing team, the team you're playing against, is working together to prevent your team from doing just that.

We see something similar in our text today. Amazing things were happening by the power of the Spirit, but there was still an opposing team who saw what was going on and mocked Jesus' first followers by accusing them of being drunk. (Parents may want to explain to their children what this means).

Jesus promised there would be opposition to him. And as we continue to learn about his mission throughout the book of Acts, we will see more and more situations in which the believers faced opposition.

Read John 16:33

- What comfort does Jesus want us to have when we are mocked or mistreated because of him?
- What is a right response when being persecuted for having faith in Jesus?

Prayer

Our Father, give us the strength to endure mistreatment that comes because we follow you. Forgive our enemies, for they do not know what they are doing. May our behavior shine a huge spotlight on your greatness, and may it provide witness to others that our greatest treasure is you, not ease or personal comfort. Thank you, God, that you have counted us worthy to bear your name.

DAY 5

The Giver is the gift

[2:2] And suddenly there came from heaven a sound like a mighty rushing wind, and it filled the entire house where they were sitting. [3] And divided tongues as of fire appeared to them and rested on each one of them. [4] And they were all filled with the Holy Spirit and began to speak in other tongues as the Spirit gave them utterance.

Jesus' first followers received an amazing gift from God—the ability to speak in other languages, so that they could reach out to different cultures of the world with the news about Jesus. How amazing is that?

But oftentimes, unfortunately, we're tempted to love God's gifts more than God himself. This is called idolatry—loving something that is not God as God. God wants us to love him more than his gifts. Consider the following story and how it helps illustrate this very important point.

A husband and wife have a very happy marriage. The husband lays down his life for his wife on a daily basis and surprises her with gifts, flowers, cards, and time away from the kids—with whom he plays, wrestles, and laughs.

As if that weren't enough, he also makes a fair amount of money and can afford to provide for all the material needs of his family, well beyond the base necessities. The kids have a huge yard to play in. His wife has a great car to drive, beautiful jewelry, a closet full of fashionable clothes. And to top it off, they regularly go on nice vacations. All is well.

Then, tragically, while away on a business trip, the husband dies in a head-on car crash with a drunk driver. In the wake of this sudden loss, the family unravels and can't figure out how to move forward.

After his death, will his family be focused on the fact he won't be around anymore to provide such great gifts? How odd would it be if one of their close friends asked them, "How are you getting along after your loss?" and they replied, "We're doing just fine. We still have all the stuff he bought us. We don't miss him at all."

Sure, those gifts were nice, but a million times stronger than their interest in those gifts is their desire to have him back. They would give up the vacations, toys, and precious jewelry just to have him back. Him and him alone. His gifts wouldn't matter in the least if they couldn't have *him*.

This is how God wants us to yearn for him. Him and him alone. Not his gifts, but him. And the greatest news in the world is that if you want him, you can have him—and no car crash will ever take him away from you.

More than any other gift, God loves to give you himself. Would you care if God were taken away but you still received all of his blessings? God is most interested in giving you himself.

What do you want most?

Prayer

Our Father, help us to love you and not just the gifts you give. We want to be deeply thankful for what you have provided, but correct us if we turn those things into idols that rob you of your right place in our hearts. We need you. Help us, please. Amen.

WEEK 4

Acts 2:14–41

DAY 1

God's word comes true

[2:14] But Peter, standing with the eleven, lifted up his voice and addressed them: "Men of Judea and all who dwell in Jerusalem, let this be known to you, and give ear to my words. [15] For these people are not drunk, as you suppose, since it is only the third hour of the day. [16] But this is what was uttered through the prophet Joel:

[17] "'And in the last days it shall be, God declares,
that I will pour out my Spirit on all flesh,
and your sons and your daughters shall prophesy,
    and your young men shall see visions,
    and your old men shall dream dreams;
[18] even on my male servants and female servants
    in those days I will pour out my Spirit, and they shall prophesy.
[19] And I will show wonders in the heavens above
    and signs on the earth below,
    blood, and fire, and vapor of smoke;
[20] the sun shall be turned to darkness
    and the moon to blood,
    before the day of the Lord comes, the great and magnificent day.
[21] And it shall come to pass that everyone who calls upon the name of the
    Lord shall be saved.'"

Have you ever been really confused? Maybe you heard a story and the details just didn't make sense, or you saw a magic trick that seems completely impossible—*How did he do that?!*

When we're confused, it really helps if someone explains what's going on, so that the world make sense again. In today's text, we see how the many onlookers who witnessed the sudden and amazing outpouring of the Holy Spirit were baffled. They wondered how Jesus' followers could suddenly start speaking different languages. Because they didn't understand, they mocked them and said they were drunk.

Then Peter, the leader of the first disciples (we'll see him in action much more as we continue in the book of Acts), stood up to explain that the disciples weren't acting crazy because they had drunk too much alcohol; rather, God's word in the Old Testament had made it clear that manifestations like this would happen when God poured out his Spirit in a new way. Peter reminded them that God keeps his word. Then he emphasized that this alone should ignite faith and rejoicing.

We can avoid the confusion by recognizing we are living in the "last days" that the prophet Joel spoke of. Repent and trust Jesus.

Read *Romans 15:13*

- According to this text, what kind of people should we be if the Spirit is in our lives?
- How can we as a family grow into truly hopeful people?

Prayer

Our Father, thank you that you have poured out your Spirit on all those who call Jesus their Lord and Savior. May we live in clarity and see mighty acts of power that give testimony to the truth of Jesus' resurrection. Use us! Let us be people who abound in hope. Help us, God. We need you. Amen.

DAY 2

What is the gospel?

[2:22] "Men of Israel, hear these words: Jesus of Nazareth, a man attested to you by God with mighty works and wonders and signs that God did through him in your midst, as you yourselves know—[23] this Jesus, delivered up according to the definite plan and foreknowledge of God, you crucified and killed by the hands of lawless men. [24] God raised him up, loosing the pangs of death, because it was not possible for him to be held by it."

Do you ever watch the news on TV? Have you ever wondered what the news really is? Isn't it just a series of announcements that describe what happened during the past twenty-four to forty-eight hours?

When we talk about "the gospel," we're referring to a similar concept. The word *gospel* simply means "good news." Imagine turning on the TV and hearing the news anchor report amazing stories of love, grace, and truth. In a sense, these would be gospel messages—news that is good.

But when Christians talk about the gospel, they're referring to the best news in all of the world: Jesus lived a perfect life by never breaking God's law, died on a cross in our place to take the punishment we should have received for all the ways we have broken God's law, and rose from the dead to prove that everything he said and did was true.

God put his ultimate stamp of approval upon Jesus through the miracle of the Resurrection. Because Jesus rose from the dead, people are forgiven and saved. God's wrath for sin no longer remains on those who trust Jesus. This is the greatest news in the world! How truly satisfying it is to know that we can be rescued and live a life that glorifies God.

If you see your need for a Savior, repent of your sins and believe Jesus is trustworthy to save you through his life, death, and resurrection. You will be saved!

In today's text, we see Peter having continued his speech to those who didn't quite know what was going on. He explained what Jesus did so that they could believe in him too and receive the Spirit of God.

Read 2 Corinthians 5:21

- Do you see how this passage reflects a short version of the gospel message?
- What do we learn about how God worked through Jesus on our behalf? (Jesus was perfect and never sinned, but God treated him as we should have been treated. Jesus is our substitute.)
- How can we be made righteous? (By being in him. We do this by coming to Jesus by faith and following him.)

Prayer

Our Father, thank you for the gospel. Thank you for the news that two thousand years ago, Jesus lived, died, and rose from the grave, so that we could be saved. May we be bold to believe it and bold to proclaim it.

DAY 3

The importance of baptism

[2:37] Now when they heard this they were cut to the heart, and said to Peter and the rest of the apostles, "Brothers, what shall we do?" [38] And Peter said to them, "Repent and be baptized every one of you in the name of Jesus Christ for the forgiveness of your sins, and you will receive the gift of the Holy Spirit. [39] For the promise is for you and for your children and for all who are far off, everyone whom the Lord our God calls to himself." [40] And with many other words he bore witness and continued to exhort them, saying, "Save yourselves from this crooked generation." [41] So those who received his word were baptized, and there were added that day about three thousand souls.

Wedding rings—are they more than just for show? Why do married people wear them?

Perhaps the most important reason is that they represent an outward symbol of an inner spiritual reality. Think about it. A wedding ring doesn't make someone married, does it? If you put on your grandma's wedding ring, does that make you married? Of course not. The ring is symbolic of something that has taken place: the wearer's status has changed from single to married.

One item that's emphasized in today's text is the practice of baptism. After hearing about Jesus' sacrifice for their sins, the crowd asked Peter what they should do next. Peter replied, "Repent and be baptized."

Yesterday we talked about the importance of becoming a Christian by believing the gospel. Today we want to talk about what happens once you are a Christian. The Bible says that once someone becomes a Christian, he or she should be baptized since baptism is the outward symbol, like a wedding ring, of a new inner spiritual reality of a new identity as a follower of Jesus.

To be baptized means to be dunked under water to symbolize, or act out, the death, burial, and resurrection of Jesus. Baptism is a picture of dying to an old life and being raised to a new life as a follower of Jesus. Since Jesus was raised from the dead, we too are given a new life as we follow him through the Spirit.

Read Acts 10:44–48

- What did Peter say should happen after the people believed the gospel and the Spirit fell on them? (They should be baptized.)

Prayer

Our Father, thank you for saving all those who come to Jesus for the forgiveness of sins. Thank you for giving us baptism, by which we're reminded of your promise that our sin has been put to death on the Cross and we have been raised to new life in you. May we see more and more people throughout the world believe in you and be baptized.

DAY 4

Cut to the heart

[2:37] Now when they heard this they were cut to the heart, and said to Peter and the rest of the apostles, "Brothers, what shall we do?" [38] And Peter said to them, "Repent and be baptized every one of you in the name of Jesus Christ for the forgiveness of your sins, and you will receive the gift of the Holy Spirit."

How can you be sure you are a Christian, a true believer in Jesus Christ?

There are many ways to know for sure, but one of the best is to consider your desires. Christians hate sin and feel remorse when they fall short of doing what pleases God. Christians love what God loves. They understand their need to repent.

Are these qualities true of you? We're not talking about sinless perfection but a desire to change. What do you desire?

People who reject Jesus tend to not mind their sin and don't feel bad about wallowing in it. But this wasn't the case with those we read about in today's Scripture passage. Instead, the people who heard Peter's message felt convicted about their sin and turned to him, asking, "What shall we do?" They sensed the urgent need to be rescued from their sin and the wrath of God.

Thankfully, Peter had a word of good news—the best news in the world: you can be saved from your sins! God has provided a way of salvation from his just wrath. How? By believing that on the cross, God punished Jesus, his own Son, to pay for your sins in order to save you. That is wonderful news!

We know the people who listened to Peter became true believers because they felt remorse for their sin and trusted the message of the gospel to save them. Is this true of you? If it is, you can know for certain that you are a Christian.

Read *Mark 1:14–15*

- What is the first indication that someone has entered into God's kingdom? (Repentance.)
- What else does Jesus say we should do? (Believe.)
- Do you see a similarity between what Jesus said in this passage and what we see in our text for today?

Prayer

Our Father, may we feel a godly sorrow for our sin. Grant us eyes to see our sin—what it really is in your sight—so that we can quickly repent and be restored to you. Thank you so much that you covered our sin through Jesus' perfect life, death, and resurrection. Amen.

DAY 5

Our God is mighty to save

> [2:41] So those who received his word were baptized, and there were added that day about three thousand souls.

God has done amazing things—there's no doubt about it. He caused a whale to swallow Jonah. He showed up in a burning bush. And let's not forget he made a donkey talk.

But perhaps God's greatest miracle appears in the passage above, where we read in verse 41 that three thousand people were saved in one day. When someone trusts Jesus for the forgiveness of their sins and chooses to follow him, it's a true miracle. Why is that? Because the human heart doesn't naturally love God all by itself. Instead, it loves to be selfish, ruling its own little kingdom of self. We enjoy making ourselves look good more than making God look good.

Self-focused love is worthless, but Jesus is worthy. And that's exactly what today's Scripture passage proves. Three thousand people! God moved in such a way that they heard the message of the gospel and responded in a massive way. Isn't that amazing?

Sometimes God works in big ways, just as this scene portrays. Peter was faithful to preach the message, and that is all we are responsible for—simply being faithful to share the best news in the world and leaving the results to God. Let's pray that God would continue to save large numbers of people, just as he did on this great day.

Read *John 1:11–13*

- Ultimately, how are people born again? (Not by the will of man, but by the will of God.)
- How can you know that you have been born again? (You have gladly received Jesus.)

Prayer
Our Father, thank you that you save. Thank you that you have power that we do not. We simply want to be faithful to share your message. Give us this boldness. Oh, how we need it! Thank you for your plan to use us in bringing those who are lost back to you. We love you. Amen.

WEEK 5

Acts 2:42–47

DAY 1

Created for community

[2:44] And all who believed were together . . .

Have you ever noticed that being alone isn't always that fun? Some people don't mind being alone for short periods of time, but most people, after a while, desire the company of others. Why is that?

The biggest reason is that God created us for community. Right after he created Adam, God said, "It is not good that the man should be alone" (Genesis 2:18). So God created Eve to provide him with companionship as his wife. We were *created* for fellowship and community. We were created for God and for one another.

We see this truth in our text today. Verse 44 says that all of Jesus' first followers were "together." Love, support, and service characterized the time they spent together.

God intends that the church should act as his main vehicle for spreading his message throughout the world. But is the gospel very attractive to those who don't know Jesus when believers aren't treating one another with kindness, love, and gentleness? Probably not. God wants his church to be a community in which its members love one another. We should be the kind of people who are so radically committed to acts of service and love that the world stands in amazement.

But you can't love those you're not spending time with. God calls us to be together, and when we are together to love each other well. We see this quality in Jesus' first followers. One way we seek to emulate their example is through our involvement at church every Sunday.

Read 1 Peter 1:22

- If we have been saved (i.e., purified by the truth), what is one way we show that our salvation is real? (Love.)
- How are we to love each other? (Sincerely and earnestly.)

Prayer

Our Father, thank you that we don't need to live in isolation, as you have created us for fellowship. Give us the grace to love sincerely and earnestly so the onlooking world will take note and want to join us in our love for you and each other. Amen.

DAY 2

Mine!

> [2:44] . . . and had all things in common. [45] And they were selling their possessions and belongings and distributing the proceeds to all, as any had need.

What is a two-year-old's favorite word? "No"? "Please"? "Da–Da"?

"Mine!" would certainly qualify. When a young child sees someone playing with a desirable toy, he or she will often proceed to rip it out of the child's hands and squeal, "Mine!"

That fact is, all kids are selfish. People are born with a sinful human nature that is naturally ungenerous and selfish. We want what we want, when we want it.

But do you notice something different in the Scripture text for today? What does it say about the first followers of Jesus? It says they were together and "had all things in common." They did not act like selfish two-year-olds by trying to keep their possessions away from others. Instead, they were willing to share "as any had need."

The gospel begins to change us when we recognize that God is not selfish with us. This helps us be generous with each other. God did the most selfless thing imaginable by giving us his Son, in order to save us from his just wrath for sin. God is the ultimate Giver, and as we see what he's done for us, we become people who love to give.

Read *2 Peter 1:2–3*

- Because of God's generosity, we have everything we need. Does God's generosity change your heart so that you want to love and serve others?

Prayer

Our Father, thank you for being so generous with us. Thank you for giving us yourself through your Son, in order to pay the price for our sins, which we could never pay. May we demonstrate we understand this by the way we live our lives, just as your first followers did. Amen.

DAY 3

A community who loved God's Word

[2:42] And they devoted themselves to the apostles' teaching.

Jesus' first followers loved God's Word, the Bible. That they were devoted to the apostles' teaching is just another way of saying they loved God's Word. The apostles taught exactly what they had heard from Jesus, and since Jesus was God, the apostles' teaching was God's Word.

Do you know why God gave us the Bible? What answers can you come up with?

There are many answers, but a great one can be found in Psalm 119:105. It reads, "Your word is a lamp to my feet and a light to my path."

Have you ever been on a dark path at night? If not, just imagine what it would be like. Would it be easy to see where you were going? Do you think you might run into a tree branch?

God says that his Word is like a light that shines on a dark path, helping you know where to go. It protects you from knocking your head on a tree branch. Isn't that a blessing?

At its core, the Bible is a story that shines God's light on a hurting world, so that all can know him. God's Word is a profound gift for his people. It's no wonder Jesus' first followers were so dedicated to it.

Read 2 Timothy 3:16–17

- Who inspired the Bible?
- What are some other reasons why God gave us the Bible?
- What is the goal of the training God provides through his Word?

Prayer

Our Father, thank you so much for giving us your Word to tell us about salvation. Thank you also that your Word is a light to our path. May we trust it by faith. Amen.

DAY 4

Breaking bread

> [2:42] And they devoted themselves to the apostles' teaching and the fellowship, to the breaking of bread and the prayers. [43] And awe came upon every soul, and many wonders and signs were being done through the apostles. [44] And all who believed were together and had all things in common. [45] And they were selling their possessions and belongings and distributing the proceeds to all, as any had need. [46] And day by day, attending the temple together and breaking bread in their homes, they received their food with glad and generous hearts.

Do you have some favorite family memories? Can you remember a fun vacation or a particularly memorable holiday or birthday?

Everyone has memories. They can make us really happy and sometimes really sad. Jesus understood the power of memory and wanted to give us a very special means for remembering him.

Before Jesus died, he wanted to establish a way for his followers to remember his sacrifice for their sins. He took a loaf of bread, something the disciples probably would have broken and eaten each day. Then he said, in essence, "Every time you break bread to eat, I want you to remember that I was broken on the cross for you." And then he took red wine, which also would have been very common to drink back then, and poured some in a cup. And the gist of his next statements was this: "Every time you drink this red wine, I want you to remember that my blood was shed to bear the wrath of God in your place."

And that is exactly what we see Jesus' first followers doing here in this text. Twice it says that they broke bread together (vv. 42, 46). Maybe you remember doing this at your church with other believers. Isn't it amazing that two thousand years later, we are still doing something that was directly commanded by Jesus?

Read *1 Corinthians 11:23–25*

- Jesus took some everyday activities, like eating and drinking, and commanded his followers to use them as a means for remembering what he had done on their behalf. Just like the body needs food everyday, we need Jesus everyday, too.

- When you take Communion, what does the bread and wine remind you of?
- Why do Christians need to be reminded of these things everyday?

Prayer

Our Father, thank you so much for giving us the sign and symbol of the Lord's Supper. We want to remember you. Help us to never forget and to live with glad hearts as we remember what Jesus has done for us. Amen.

DAY 5

God grows the church

[2:42] And they devoted themselves to the apostles' teaching and the fellowship, to the breaking of bread and the prayers. [43] And awe came upon every soul, and many wonders and signs were being done through the apostles. [44] And all who believed were together and had all things in common. [45] And they were selling their possessions and belongings and distributing the proceeds to all, as any had need. [46] And day by day, attending the temple together and breaking bread in their homes, they received their food with glad and generous hearts, [47] praising God and having favor with all the people. And the Lord added to their number day by day those who were being saved.

Are you growing any taller? How do you know? Do you have any idea how much you've grown in the last year?

Why do you think you are able to grow? Do you think you'd be able to grow very well if you didn't eat? How about if you didn't sleep? Do flowers grow very well if they're never in the sunshine?

Of course not. In order to grow, living things must be exposed to the right conditions. Kids require healthy food and adequate sleep. Flowers need good light and plenty of water. In the same way, the church must be exposed to the right conditions, so that it can grow in a way that honors God.

Do you know what God loves to use to grow his church? He loves exactly what we see in our text for this week. Can you remember what Jesus' first followers were devoted to?

They were devoted to God's Word, and they loved to pray, to give, and to remember Jesus in communion. And they were full of the Holy Spirit.

These are the exact conditions that create growth in the church. God wouldn't want to bring the unsaved to his church if people there never opened their Bibles and hated each other by acting with arrogance and selfishness. Would you like to go to a church like that?

Thankfully, we don't see this kind of picture painted among Jesus' first followers. That's why God was pleased to grow that church.

Read *Matthew 16:18*

- Who builds the church?
- Will anything stop this building process?

Prayer

Our Father, thank you so much for building your church. We want to be the kind of church that pleases you. May we be quick to repent in areas where we fall short of your ways. Thank you for the forgiveness that is found in Jesus' life, death, and resurrection. May we continually stand in awe of what you have done to save us. Amen.

WEEK 6

Acts 3:1–10

DAY 1

Money can't buy miracles

[3:1] Now Peter and John were going up to the temple at the hour of prayer, the ninth hour. [2] And a man lame from birth was being carried, whom they laid daily at the gate of the temple that is called the Beautiful Gate to ask alms of those entering the temple. [3] Seeing Peter and John about to go into the temple, he asked to receive alms. [4] And Peter directed his gaze at him, as did John, and said, "Look at us." [5] And he fixed his attention on them, expecting to receive something from them. [6] But Peter said, "I have no silver and gold, but what I do have I give to you. In the name of Jesus Christ of Nazareth, rise up and walk!" [7] And he took him by the right hand and raised him up, and immediately his feet and ankles were made strong. [8] And leaping up he stood and began to walk, and entered the temple with them, walking and leaping and praising God.

Have you ever heard the phrase, "Money makes the world go 'round"? Do you think it's true? What could be more important than money?

In our text for today, we see a man who needs money because he is very poor and can't walk. Most likely he would not have been able to get a good job. So he resorted to begging. Have you ever seen someone on the street asking for money? The scenes are similar.

But some things in life are better than money—like Jesus. Having him in your life is better than having all of the money in the world. Knowing Jesus doesn't mean life will be without problems, but it does mean we can rest assured that he is with us now and will be with us in eternity. And that is by far the greatest possession in the world.

In today's Scripture passage, we see how Jesus' first followers, Peter and John, helped the poor man understand this truth. They taught him that Jesus was worthy to be trusted, far more than silver or gold. By the power of God's Spirit, they commanded this lame man to stand up and walk. Miraculously, he jumped to his feet!

Do you believe God can do miracles? He can, and he wants to demonstrate his power through us, so that the whole world will know he is powerful, loving, and worthy to be trusted.

Read *Matthew 5:14–16*

- Why does God want us to do good works?
- What are some good works that you could do to help others?

Prayer

Our Father, help us believe that knowing you is better than having all the money in the world. Like Peter and John, may we glorify you through this belief. Amen.

DAY 2

Enthusiastic praise

[3:8] And leaping up he stood and began to walk, and entered the temple with them, walking and leaping and praising God.

Have you ever attended the final minutes of a game, where it was down to the wire, and your favorite team at the last second scored the point that won it? What happened?

The fans freaked out, right? They were jumping up and down and giving high fives while screaming and yelling with joy.

Why do they act like this? Isn't it because we often express extreme happiness in physical ways that engage our bodies? Didn't the man in our text have reason to jump up and down with joy? Can you imagine being lame your whole life, and then in an instant God heals you? What would you do?

God created us with physical bodies, and he wants us to use them to praise him for what he's done. Sometimes when we sing to God, we raise our hands to show surrender, or we bow down to show humility. Sometimes we cry to show remorse, repentance, or sadness, and sometimes we smile and laugh to express our joy.

God wants us to be like this man who was healed. May we express our thanks and praise in ways that appropriately acknowledge what he has done.

Read *Psalm 95:1–7*

- In what ways does the psalmist exhort us to show physical expression in light of what God has done?

Prayer

Our Father, may we not be too proud to show how much we love you. May we show more praise for you than what we show at a football game or soccer match. You have done the greatest thing in the world by saving us from your wrath. May we recognize this to a greater degree and display it in our lives. Amen.

DAY 3

Walking and praising

[3:9] And all the people saw him walking and praising God.

The phrase "What do you say?" is often asked by parents who are training their children to use "please" when asking for something. What is the heart behind this instructive question from parents to children?

It's to train them to be thankful and have good manners. When you receive something as a gift, the appropriate response should be thanks and praise.

Think about it like this: when you receive a gift on your birthday or at Christmas, do you immediately think, *Wow. They gave me this gift. I just be really awesome!*?

Of course not. The usual response is to thank the person who gave the gift and also to think very highly of the giver. *Wow. She gave me just what I needed. She's so generous and kind!*

This is the same response we need to show God when he blesses us. He wants us to recognize that all good gifts come from him. We should praise our heavenly Father and not think so much about ourselves when we receive good gifts from him.

In today's Scripture passage, we see this kind of response modeled in the man who was healed. He was truly thankful, and for that reason he gave significant praise to God. He wasn't thinking about himself; he was thinking about God.

Read *James 1:17*

- Where do all good things ultimately come from?

DAILY DEVOTIONS

Prayer

Our Father, may we recognize that you are the Giver of all good things and that you are not one to withhold them from us. Help us believe that you will give us everything we need—and much more. Amen.

DAY 4

Taking notice of God's work

> [3:9] And all the people saw him walking and praising God, [10] and recognized him as the one who sat at the Beautiful Gate of the temple, asking for alms. And they were filled with wonder and amazement at what had happened to him.

Did you know that God's work in your life is not just for you? He loves it when you recognize his work in your life. But do you know what else he loves? When other people recognize his work in your life.

In today's Scripture text, did anyone notice the lame man praising God for his healing? What was their response?

God loves to makes himself famous. He wants his glory to spread through the whole world "as the waters cover the sea" (Isaiah 11:9).

Read 1 Chronicles 16:8

- Do you think it is important for us to publicly display what God has done in our lives?
- Can you think of ways you can do that yourself or as a family?
- What has God done in your life, and what can you do, so that people take notice and are filled with "wonder and amazement" at his works?

Prayer

Our Father, please use our lives to display the greatness of who you are and what you can do. Help us be willing, with boldness and joy, to show and tell what you have done. Amen.

DAY 5

In the name of . . . !

[3:6] But Peter said, "I have no silver and gold, but what I do have
I give to you. In the name of Jesus Christ of Nazareth, rise up and
walk!" [7] And he took him by the right hand and raised him up, and
immediately his feet and ankles were made strong.

Have you ever heard the phrase, "Stop, in the name of the law!"?

We don't hear it very often these days in TV and movies, but years ago it was
heard often. A character would be robbing a bank or hurting someone, and then the
hero would jump in and yell, "Stop, in the name of the law!"

The hero is compelling the antagonist to stop his crime by appealing to a higher
order. "In the name of . . ." invokes the authority of something. In this case, it's the
authority of the laws of the land.

Peter and John used a similar expression in today's text: "In the name of Jesus
Christ of Nazareth, rise up and walk!" Knowing they didn't have authority in and of
themselves, they called upon Jesus' authority to do this amazing miracle. Jesus, by
the power of his Spirit, gave them the power to heal.

These are not magic words a person can say anytime to get what he or she
wants. Moving in God's power is not like summoning a genie by rubbing a magic
lamp. But sometimes God loves to display his glory and power through his people in
miraculous ways. We should ask him to do it for the sake of his name being known
in our world today.

Read *Colossians 3:17*

- What things are we supposed to do "in the name of the Lord"?
  (Everything—word and deed.)
- What does this verse have to do with today's text from Acts? (Peter and
  John were under the authority of Jesus. All of life is to be lived under the
  authority of King Jesus.)

Prayer

Our Father, thank you that you are powerful to heal and save. May your name
be known by more and more people throughout our world. May you continue to
do marvelous works to draw attention to who you are and your power over all of
creation. Amen.

WEEK 7

Acts 3:11–26

DAY 1

Peter, the coward no more

[3:11] While he clung to Peter and John, all the people, utterly astounded, ran together to them in the portico called Solomon's. [12] And when Peter saw it he addressed the people: "Men of Israel, why do you wonder at this, or why do you stare at us, as though by our own power or piety we have made him walk? [13] The God of Abraham, the God of Isaac, and the God of Jacob, the God of our fathers, glorified his servant Jesus, whom you delivered over and denied in the presence of Pilate, when he had decided to release him. [14] But you denied the Holy and Righteous One, and asked for a murderer to be granted to you, [15] and you killed the Author of life, whom God raised from the dead. To this we are witnesses. [16] And his name—by faith in his name—has made this man strong whom you see and know, and the faith that is through Jesus has given the man this perfect health in the presence of you all."

In today's text, we see Peter being very bold. He says some very hard things to his audience. In your own words, can you describe what he said?

Read Luke 22:54–62

- Would you regard Peter as courageous and bold based on the text that we just read? There was a time when Peter was scared to be identified with Jesus. In fact, in Luke 22:54–62, Peter denied even knowing Jesus—three times! But in Acts he is very bold and has no problem being identified with Jesus and challenging the people who were listening.
- What do you think caused the change in Peter? What huge event took place right after Jesus died? (The Resurrection.)
- Do you think you would have acted differently than Peter? If you saw your leader being dragged off to be murdered on a cross, might you be a little scared too? What if he rose from the dead three days later and spent lots of time talking with you. Would it not completely amaze you and cause you

to believe everything he said? All of these amazing events happened to Peter. The Resurrection changed his life. He was a new man because Jesus had risen from the dead, proving he was God. And Peter knew it for sure.

Prayer

Our Father, would you please make us bold like Peter? May we, too, believe in your resurrection and stand in awe of it, so that our lives can be changed. We love you. Amen.

DAY 2

God's work, our witness

[3:11] While he clung to Peter and John, all the people, utterly astounded, ran together to them in the portico called Solomon's. [12] And when Peter saw it he addressed the people: "Men of Israel, why do you wonder at this, or why do you stare at us, as though by our own power or piety we have made him walk? [13] The God of Abraham, the God of Isaac, and the God of Jacob, the God of our fathers, glorified his servant Jesus, whom you delivered over and denied in the presence of Pilate, when he had decided to release him. [14] But you denied the Holy and Righteous One, and asked for a murderer to be granted to you, [15] and you killed the Author of life, whom God raised from the dead. To this we are witnesses. [16] And his name—by faith in his name—has made this man strong whom you see and know, and the faith that is through Jesus has given the man this perfect health in the presence of you all."

Do you know what a *witness* is?

Sometimes we use that term to describe someone who saw a crime take place. If you were a witness to a crime, a policeman might ask questions about what you saw to help solve the case. A witness is someone who saw something and simply speaks about what he or she observed.

In the text for today, Peter is a type of witness. What was he a witness to? As we talked about yesterday, Peter was first and foremost a witness to Jesus' life, death, and resurrection. He was a changed man, transformed from a coward to a courageous preacher. Witnessing Jesus risen from the grave gave Peter power to no longer fear death; it gave him a passion for telling everyone about what he saw and knew to be true.

What comprised the content about which he spoke? The message of the gospel—the life, death, and resurrection of Jesus. We see very clearly in our text that the gospel is God's work, and it's our job to tell others about what we've seen God do in our lives. We are the witnesses; we simply tell people about what God has done. He gets the glory when we tell the story.

Read *John 15:26–27*

- In this text, Jesus is speaking to his disciples. Why does Jesus say they will "bear witness"? (Because they have been with him.)
- We haven't been with Jesus in the same way the disciples were with him, but can we still "bear witness"? How? (Through the testimony of the Bible, through miracles in our lives, etc.)

Prayer

Our Father, thank you so much for what you have done in history. May we give you glory by telling your story. We believe you have done mighty things in the past and continue to do mighty things today. Thank you that your mightiest work was conquering our sin and raising Jesus from the dead. Amen.

DAY 3

His power, not ours

> [3:12] And when Peter saw it he addressed the people: "Men of Israel, why do you wonder at this, or why do you stare at us, as though by our own power or piety we have made him walk?"

> [16] "And his name—by faith in his name—has made this man strong whom you see and know, and the faith that is through Jesus has given the man this perfect health in the presence of you all."

A touchdown dance—have you ever seen one?

When a football player catches the ball in the end zone, his team scores six points. So when it happens, there is cause for celebration. But oftentimes the player who catches the ball forgets it was a team effort. He stands up and dances around in celebration, pointing his finger at his chest and yelling something like, "I'm the man! I'm the best! Check me out!" At that moment, he thinks all the credit for the touchdown should go to him.

What do you think about that?

He's forgetting that the other players on his team helped make the touchdown happen, isn't he? Shouldn't he give credit to the other players as well?

In today's text, we see Peter giving credit where credit is due. Isn't it cool that after God used Peter to heal the lame man, Peter didn't boast, saying "Hey, check me out. I'm the man!"? What *did* Peter say?

He gave all of the credit to God's power, not his own. God wants us to remember where our power comes from. He knows that our greatest joy is found in reliance upon him rather than ourselves.

Read *2 Corinthians 4:7*

- Do you think it would be easy to break a clay jar? (Yes, very easy; clay is not very strong.)
- Why does God use weak things? (He gets the glory for picking up the pieces. It forces us to rely on him when things break.)

Prayer

Our Father, may we know where our power comes from. When we are weak, we know that you are strong. When you work through us, help us remind people that our power comes from you and is meant for your glory, not ours. Give us this boldness. Amen.

DAY 4

You're going the wrong way!

[3:17] "And now, brothers, I know that you acted in ignorance, as did also your rulers. [18] But what God foretold by the mouth of all the prophets, that his Christ would suffer, he thus fulfilled. [19] Repent therefore, and turn back, that your sins may be blotted out, [20] that times of refreshing may come from the presence of the Lord."

A two-way street. Picture cars driving in separate lanes and going in opposite directions. Most roads are like this. But on a one-way street, cars must travel in the same direction.

What would happen if you suddenly realized you were driving the wrong way on a one-way street? You'd need to turn around quickly or risk getting in a pretty bad accident, right?

That's kind of what Peter said to the people in today's text. He told them to turn around and go the other way. This is what repentance means—saying you're sorry for your sins, then turning your life around so you're going in the opposite direction, away from sin and toward righteousness.

What did Peter say would happen if we turned away from sin—if we repented? If we repented? He said God would forgive us and blot out, or erase, our sin so that it is not counted against us. Isn't that good news? The way of forgiveness is through repentance.

Read *1 John 1:8–9*

- Are we sinless or sinful? (Sinful.)
- What happens when we confess our sin? (He forgives us.)
- Are we still dirty, or are we clean in God's sight? (Clean.)
- Are there any sins that you want to confess right now?

Prayer

Our Father, thank you so much for sending your Son to forgive our sins when we turn from them and repent. May we show the same grace to others when they sin against us. We need your help. Amen.

DAY 5

There is a day coming . . .

> [3:19] "Repent therefore, and turn back, that your sins may be blotted out, [20] that times of refreshing may come from the presence of the Lord, and that he may send the Christ appointed for you, Jesus, [21] whom heaven must receive until the time for restoring all the things about which God spoke by the mouth of his holy prophets long ago."

A few weeks ago, we talked about how Jesus ascended to heaven after being raised from the dead and spending some time with his first followers. Do you remember that he promised to return?

He did, and he will.

Peter talked about it in our verse for today. He said that "heaven must receive

[him] until the time for restoring all the things about which God spoke by the mouth of his holy prophets."

This means there is coming a day when the sadness in our world will turn to joy. This is great news. If you have repented of your sins and are following Jesus, his return is the greatest thing in the world because he will make right everything that is wrong. If you haven't repented, his return is bad news, since he will punish those who don't love him by sending them away from him forever.

This is why Peter told his audience to repent, and it's why it's important for us to repent. God has to punish sin. It would be wrong for a parent to ignore a brother who's beating up his little sister, wouldn't it? When people do things that are wrong, God must get involved in order to bring discipline and punish wrongdoers. Otherwise, he wouldn't be a good God, would he?

But the greatest news in the world is that after dealing with sin for one final time, Jesus will make all things new, and those who love him will live in this perfect world forever.

Read *Revelation 21:1–5*

- This is a description of what eternal life with Jesus will be like. What is good about it? What do you look forward to?

Prayer

Our Father, thank you for giving us such beautiful promises, so that we might have hope. We can't wait for all things to be made new. Do it soon, Jesus.

WEEK 8

Acts 4:1–22

DAY 1

Opposition

> [4:1] And as they were speaking to the people, the priests and the captain of the temple and the Sadducees came upon them, [2] greatly annoyed because they were teaching the people and proclaiming in Jesus the resurrection from the dead. [3] And they arrested them and put them in custody until the next day, for it was already evening.

There will always be people who don't like Jesus. Jesus himself promised this would be the case. Why do you think this reality exists?

A major reason is that people don't like hearing that they're wrong. We see this in our text today. The Sadducees and priests didn't like what Jesus' first followers were preaching because it was different from their own message. In essence, it demonstrates that the Jewish leaders were wrong. And they hated those who claimed they were wrong.

Do you like hearing you are wrong? Most people don't.

The Christian message does just that: it states there is something desperately wrong with humanity. We have broken God's laws. We are sinners. We need someone to save us from our sin because we can't save ourselves. It's interesting, though, that most people believe they can redeem themselves by doing good things. They think, *If I can be "just good enough," then God will overlook the bad things I've done.*

But the message of Christianity is that it's not possible to do enough good things to earn God's forgiveness. Instead, someone else must do good works for us and incur the punishment for our sins. This is exactly what Jesus did when he lived a perfect life and died on the cross to bear the penalty we should have paid.

But there will always be people who hate this message. Don't be afraid, though. Jesus is with you by the power of the Holy Spirit, and he will help you.

Read *2 Timothy 3:12*

- What is one of the marks of godliness? (Persecution/opposition.)

DAILY DEVOTIONS

Prayer

Our Father, give us the strength to love those who don't love you. Would you save them? Help us to trust you when we are persecuted and to pray for those who hate us because of you. We need your help, and you have promised to give it. Thank you so much. Amen.

DAY 2

Hearing and believing

> [4:4] But many of those who had heard the word believed, and the number of the men came to about five thousand.

Peanut butter and jelly. A baseball and a glove. Frodo and Sam. These are examples of two things that usually go together. Can you think of more?

When it comes to saving faith, two very important things that always go together are hearing and believing. We see that in our text for today: "many of those who had heard the word believed."

In order to become a Christian, you must hear the message of the gospel, and you must believe it. It's not enough to just say you know certain things are true. Many people know the truth about Jesus but still hate him—like the religious leaders who were persecuting Peter and John. They knew that Jesus had risen from the dead, but they still hated him.

What is required is a certain kind of knowing. It's knowing that the gospel isn't just for other people, but for you, too. It's not just knowing facts about Jesus; rather, it's knowing Jesus intimately and loving him.

Read Romans 10:13–14

- How do people get saved? (Hearing and calling on the name of the Lord.)
- Is there someone you know who needs to hear the gospel?

Prayer

Our Father, may we see in our day what your first followers saw. We want many, many people to hear the gospel and believe it. May you draw them to yourself. Please use us as your message bearers. Amen.

DAY 3

The Holy Spirit helps us when persecuted

[4:8] Then Peter, filled with the Holy Spirit, said to them, "Rulers of the people and elders, [9] if we are being examined today concerning a good deed done to a crippled man, by what means this man has been healed, [10] let it be known to all of you and to all the people of Israel that by the name of Jesus Christ of Nazareth, whom you crucified, whom God raised from the dead—by him this man is standing before you well.

How do you feel when you know someone is angry with you? Are you a little scared?

It's never fun, but unfortunately, from time to time, it's just part of life. People don't always get along, and at times it can turn ugly.

Jesus also promised that our faith in him would provoke others to anger. We see that in our text for today. Peter was doing exactly what God wanted, but he faced extreme pressure from powerful people who didn't love Jesus and asked him to defend his actions. What was Peter's response? Was anyone there to help him?

When we are persecuted for our faith, we don't have to fear. Why? Because, as this Scripture passage demonstrates, God will give us the words we need. The Holy Spirit filled Peter with God's power in that moment, and he said exactly what God wanted.

Isn't it comforting to know that when we face hard things from people who don't love Jesus, he promises to be with us?

Read *Luke 21:12–15*

- Why does Jesus say we shouldn't worry about what to say when we face opposition? (He will give us the words to speak.)

Prayer

Our Father, thank you that you promise to be with us when we are persecuted for your sake. May you use the words you give us to bring honor to your name, and may some even be saved because of them. Help us to be faithful. Amen.

DAY 4

No other name

> [4:12] "And there is salvation in no one else, for there is no other name under heaven given among men by which we must be saved."

You likely already know there are millions and millions of people on Earth, but if you were to guess an actual number, what would it be? According to Google, the number is around seven billion.

Do you know that a few billion of these people have never heard of Jesus? A few billion others think there are ways to be saved from God's wrath and have eternal life apart from Jesus.

It's very sad but very true. A large majority of the world does not know about Jesus. Still others have flat out rejected him.

If our verse for today is true, then what should we do about this problem?

We need people to go into all of the world to spread the news about Jesus. He is the only way, and we must share him with those who have never heard.

Read John 14:6

- How do people get to the Father? (Through Jesus.)
- Is there any other way? (No, only through Jesus.)
- What if I am a really good person? ("Being good" is not the issue. Can you be perfect? Only Jesus can save because he lived a perfect life. That perfection is credited to us when we come to him by faith.)

Prayer

Our Father, thank you that you are able to save. We so desperately need a Savior. Thank you that you have made it clear that salvation is found only in you. May we be eager to tell others this amazing news. Amen.

DAY 5

Just a couple of normal guys

> [4:13] Now when they saw the boldness of Peter and John, and perceived that they were uneducated, common men, they were astonished. And they recognized that they had been with Jesus.

Does God seem to pick certain types of people to accomplish his purposes? Consider some of the characters in the Bible whom God used to do mighty things:

- David was just a simple shepherd boy, yet God used him to slay a giant.
- Jonah was a grumpy prophet, but God used him to lead a whole city to repentance.
- Moses was prone to temper tantrums, and he didn't speak very well; still, God used him to defeat the most powerful man in the world and set his people free from slavery.

God loves to use ordinary people for extraordinary tasks. We see that as well in our text for today: Peter and John were just a couple of normal dudes who surrendered to God and were filled with the power of his Spirit. God was with them, and the people took notice!

Do you think you could do the same?

Read Matthew 28:18–20

- What comforting promise is given at the end of this text? (God will always be with us.)
- How does that change how we view our mission to tell others about Jesus? (It should give us courage and boldness.)
- Is this verse just for people who are really smart or talented? (No, it's for all who love Jesus.)

Prayer

Our Father, thank you that you promise to be with us and empower us. Oftentimes we feel so weak and unable to do your will. We are just normal people. But we know that you are not a normal God. We know and trust that you have empowered us and will continue to glorify yourself through our lives.

WEEK 9

Acts 4:23–31

DAY 1

Responding to opposition

> [4:23] When they were released, they went to their friends and reported
> what the chief priests and the elders had said to them. [24] And when
> they heard it, they lifted their voices together to God.

When someone is angry with you or is opposing you, what is your first response?
Run? Fight?

In today's text, how did Jesus' first followers respond to severe persecution at
the hands of the religious leaders? Prayer—they knew their only source of power
was God himself.

God loves to pour out his power when we pray because he loves to demonstrate
how great he is. He doesn't like it too much when we try to make people think we
are great. But he loves it when we help people see that he is great. When we pray, it
shows we need help, strength, and wisdom. But most of all, it shows that we need
him. And when we pray, it shows we believe that God is worthy to be trusted and
powerful enough to help.

There is no greater time to pray than when people are opposing us like they
opposed Jesus' first followers. May we follow their lead and respond as they did. They
didn't fight back, they didn't run, and they didn't lie. They prayed!

Read Romans 12:12

- What three things does God love to see his people doing? (Rejoicing, being
  patient, and praying.)
- Are we to pray only when we face opposition? (No, we should pray
  constantly.)

Prayer

Our Father, thank you so much for the privilege of prayer. Help us remember to
come to you as our only true help when we face any kind of opposition. Amen.

DAY 2

Spreading the word

> [4:23] When they were released, they went to their friends and reported what the chief priests and the elders had said to them.

When in trouble, some people try to toughen up and figure things out all by themselves. When feelings are hurt, some try to hide their emotions, pretending like everything is fine.

Do you think this is good? Why or why not?

Part of the reason God has given the church to his people is so they can help share one another's burdens by praying and helping, just like we read about in yesterday's devotion. Doesn't this sound better than just trying to do everything by yourself?

This principle is clearly portrayed in today's Scripture passage. When Jesus' first followers received some harsh persecution, they didn't bottle it up. The text says that "they went to their friends" and told them what had happened. This is exactly what God wants us to do. May we follow their lead and share our burdens with one another.

Read Galatians 6:2

- What fulfills God's law? (Bearing one another's burdens.)
- Are there any burdens you have that you can talk about as a family?

Prayer

Our Father, thank you that you hear us when we come to you with our problems and burdens. May we love each other enough to do that together as well. Give us words of life to bless your people. Give us grace to selflessly listen and offer compassion to those who are hurting. May we be like your first followers and be eager to pray with one another. Amen.

DAY 3

Boldness

[4:29] "And now, Lord, look upon their threats and grant to your servants to continue to speak your word with all boldness, [30] while you stretch out your hand to heal, and signs and wonders are performed through the name of your holy servant Jesus."

Shhhhhhhhhhh!

It's likely that every one of us has received this command at some point in our lives. If you talk loudly in a movie theatre, those sitting around you will probably ask you to "keep it down." If you yell in the library, someone will surely come over and ask you to take it down a notch. And if you're noisy when the baby is sleeping, you'll certainly receive a quick reprimand to quiet your voice.

It's good to keep quiet in these types of scenarios, but it's certainly not acceptable to keep quiet in every situation. When a car is about to barrel into someone who's walking across the street, yelling "Look out!" is actually quite the loving thing to do.

Jesus' disciples demonstrated something similar in our today's text. Even in the face of opposition, they knew God didn't want them to keep quiet when there was so much at stake. To do so wouldn't demonstrate God's love. So they prayed for boldness in declaring that Jesus was the way—the only way—to eternal life.

Read Colossians 4:3–4

- Paul was in prison when he wrote this verse. What does he ask people to do for him? (Pray.)
- What are they to pray for? (That Paul would be bold and clear.)
- Does this characterize the kind of people we have been learning about in Acts? (Yes!)
- Is there anyone in your life with whom you would like to share Jesus, but perhaps you hesitate because you are a bit afraid and need to pray for boldness?

Prayer

Our Father, would you make us bold like Paul and your first followers in Acts? We need your help. We're tempted to be quiet and scared. May you provide us with a huge vision of yourself that is so inspiring that we could never keep quiet, even when we are frightened. Amen.

DAY 4

God had a plan

> [4:27] "for truly in this city there were gathered together against your holy servant Jesus, whom you anointed, both Herod and Pontius Pilate, along with the Gentiles and the peoples of Israel, [28] to do whatever your hand and your plan had predestined to take place."

Jesus' death on the cross was not a mistake, and it was not a surprise. It was planned by God long, long ago as the means by which he would save his people from their sins.

Do you think Herod, Pontius Pilate, and others who opposed Jesus and wanted him dead knew about God's plan?

No. They didn't think Jesus was God's servant. They thought he was crazy or a liar.

Isn't it amazing that God can accomplish his purposes even though people hate him and oppose him? Our God is very, very powerful. He will do as he pleases, even if we don't love him. We see that clearly in this text.

There were many people who hated Jesus and thought by killing him they were doing God's work. But little did they know God had planned they would kill Jesus all along. Jesus' enemies did what they wanted, but through their evil actions, God also did what he wanted—accomplish salvation for all those who love him. Isn't that amazing?

Read Psalm 115:3

- Can anyone stop God's plan? (No.)
- Can God only do some of the things he wants to do? (No. He can do anything he wants. He is God.)

Prayer

Our Father, you are so powerful. Your plans can never be thwarted. Knowing that nothing can stop you helps us trust you. We rest secure in your control and love. Amen.

DAY 5

God answers prayer

[4:31] And when they had prayed, the place in which they were gathered together was shaken, and they were all filled with the Holy Spirit and continued to speak the word of God with boldness.

Do you notice what happened when Peter, John, and their friends prayed? Two very important things took place.

They were (1) filled with the Holy Spirit, and (2) they continued to speak with boldness.

Do you remember what they had asked for a few verses before this passage? They had prayed for boldness (v. 29), and our text today clearly shows how God granted that request in answer to their prayers! They did not keep quiet but continued to speak with boldness.

When we are filled with the Holy Spirit, we have to talk about Jesus because the main job of the Holy Spirit is to draw attention to the greatness of Jesus and what he did in his life, death, and resurrection.

Isn't it great knowing that God loves to answer prayer? He especially loves to do so when our prayers are completely in line with the things he loves. We see that in today's text. God loves to empower his people by the Spirit to tell other people boldly about Jesus.

Read 2 Corinthians 3:12

- If we have hope in God, what does that produce in us? (Boldness.)
- Are there ways you want to grow in boldness? How can you do that? (Prayer is a good place to start.)

Prayer

Our Father, thank you so much for answering our prayers when we ask for things that you love. May our heart be your heart. May our desires be your desires. May our loves be your loves. Please give us more of your Holy Spirit, so that we too can be bold like the people in our text today. Amen.

WEEK 10

Acts 4:32–5:11

DAY 1

No needs

[4:34] There was not a needy person among them.

Our world is full of needs. Just turn on the TV and you'll hear painful stories of those who have many needs. Children without parents. People who can't find enough to eat or who are dying from lack of clean water. Wars. Broken lives. People stealing from one another. The list goes on and on.

This reality is part of what it means to live in a world full of sin. There will always be people who have needs that are never filled in this life. It's also why we long for Jesus to return soon and redeem all of the sadness. We pray for his kingdom to manifest on earth as it is in heaven.

In light of all of the brokenness, isn't it amazing to read in our text today that in the community of Jesus' first followers "there was not a needy person among them"? When God's Spirit infects a community, its members become consumed not with their own needs but the needs of others.

Isn't this how Jesus treats us? He laid aside his own needs for the sake of others. We reflect his character and glory when we focus on others and not on ourselves. It's the best way to live, and it brings the most joy.

Read *Philippians 2:1–8*

- How does this text show us that Jesus was not selfish? (He became a servant even unto death.)
- How can you grow in becoming more of a servant in your family, at school, or at church?
- Are there needs in your sphere of influence that you could meet or address as a family?

Prayer

Our Father, thank you for meeting our ultimate need in the life, death, and resurrection of Jesus. Thank you for saving us from wrath. May you stir in us a desire to reflect you and your selflessness as we seek to meet the needs of others in our church family and those outside our church family. We want to do this for your glory. Please use us. Amen.

DAY 2

Willing to sell it all for the mission

> [4:36] Thus Joseph, who was also called by the apostles Barnabas (which means son of encouragement), a Levite, a native of Cyprus, [37] sold a field that belonged to him and brought the money and laid it at the apostles' feet.

What do you like to spend your money on? Toys? Games? Apps? What's the first thing that comes to mind? What do you find most valuable?

When the New Testament was written about two thousand years ago, money was in use in much the same way it is today. For example, people used different types of coins that represented different values. People also measured wealth through ownership of land or property. Since many people in Bible times were poor, owning a piece of property meant you were probably quite rich. Their world wasn't like what we know here in the United States, where most have enough food to eat, a place to live, a car to drive, and clothes to wear.

This is what makes today's Scripture portion so remarkable. We read that Barnabas sold his land and gave the proceeds to the church. Why do you think he gave such a significant gift?

Probably because he valued God's kingdom and mission more than he valued the property he owned. Even though it could have made him very rich, he chose instead to invest in the riches God gives—riches like forgiveness, community, purpose, and peace. The world doesn't understand this, but as God's children, we know that his gifts are much more deeply satisfying and valuable than being monetarily rich.

Read Luke 18:18–27

- What is the difference between Barnabas and the rich ruler? (One is selfish, and the other is generous.)
- Does being generous save us, or is it a reflection of the fact that we have been saved? (Clearly the latter. Good works don't save. They are the fruit of those who love Jesus. Jesus was revealing the rich ruler's own heart to him—that he loved money more than God.)

Prayer

Our Father, thank you that we don't have to tightly grip our possessions because you promise to give us everything we need. May we love you more than our stuff. Purge our hearts of idols. Make us willing to give everything we have for the sake of your mission. Thank you for the promise that we can't outgive you. We believe it. Help our unbelief. Amen.

DAY 3

Lying

[5:1] But a man named Ananias, with his wife Sapphira, sold a piece of property, [2] and with his wife's knowledge he kept back for himself some of the proceeds and brought only a part of it and laid it at the apostles' feet. [3] But Peter said, "Ananias, why has Satan filled your heart to lie to the Holy Spirit and to keep back for yourself part of the proceeds of the land? [4] While it remained unsold, did it not remain your own? And after it was sold, was it not at your disposal? Why is it that you have contrived this deed in your heart? You have not lied to man but to God." [5] When Ananias heard these words, he fell down and breathed his last. And great fear came upon all who heard of it. [6] The young men rose and wrapped him up and carried him out and buried him.

Yesterday we saw the beauty of Barnabas' selflessness. He owned some property and sold it for the sake of the mission of the church. Today we encounter another story about selling property—but with a very different twist.

Have you ever told a lie? Be honest. You wouldn't want to lie about lying!

Jesus was the only person who ever lived who never told a lie. Everyone is guilty of lying at some point in life. Thankfully we know that we can be forgiven for this sin.

In today's text, we see that Ananias lied to the Holy Spirit about the money he gave to the church for its mission. Do you know why lying is such a big deal? Because it destroys relationships. If you belonged to a group of people who lied to each other all of the time, do you think you would feel comfortable? Do you think you would feel close to them?

Remember what we have learned up to this point from the book of Acts. One of the most prominent themes has been the close community shared by Jesus' earliest followers. Their great love for one another and strong relationships carried them through harsh persecution. But do you think they could have continued to thrive if lying broke out among them?

Absolutely not. It would devastate the unity and love shared by Jesus' first followers, causing them to become very weak.

So God did something about it. He removed Ananias and his wife from their midst for good. Because the purity of this community was so important, he didn't allow anything to threaten it.

Read *Ephesians 4:25*

- For what reason are we to put away falsehood and speak truth? (Because we are a family. Families don't work well when members lie to one another.)

Prayer

Our Father, thank you that we know you always tell the truth. Protect us from the enemy, Satan, the father of lies. May the manner in which we speak to one another glorify you, for the sake of the purity of your church. Amen.

DAY 4

The fear of the Lord

[5:11] And great fear came upon the whole church and upon all who heard of these things.

When was the last time you were really scared? What happened?

In today's text, we see the people responding to what happened to Ananias and his wife in a distinct way. It says "great fear" came upon them. Do you think they were crying, shaking, and screaming as some people do when watching a scary movie?

The word *fear* carries different connotations, and when the Bible speaks about it, it usually means something more like the word *reverence*. What does this mean?

Probably something like the feeling a child gets while watching his mom or dad discipline a sibling. It's a time to be serious, not silly, quiet, not loud and crazy. It's definitely not a time to run up to your dad and try to tickle him.

Can you imagine meeting the president of the United States? Do you think you would run up to him and kick him in the shins or spit out your gum on him? Of course not. That would be very disrespectful. If you met the president, you would act in a certain manner because of who he is. You would be showing him reverence in that way.

So when the Bible says we should "fear" God, it means we should revere him by showing him honor and respect because we recognize how wonderful and powerful he is. In today's text, we see Jesus' first followers demonstrating this principle, and it was very honoring to God.

Read *Psalm 111:10*

- What do we receive when we fear the Lord? (Understanding and wisdom.)
- Why do you think this is the case?

Prayer

Our Father, thank you that you have revealed yourself to us. May we approach you in ways that honor you. You are a truly awesome God, and we stand in awe of who you are and what you have done. Amen.

DAY 5

Fear of others

[5:11] And great fear came upon the whole church and upon all who heard of these things.

Has anyone ever made a mean face at you for no reason or been unloving to you even when you've been really nice? Were you worried about what that other person thought about you? Or have you ever done something unpleasing to God in an attempt to get someone to like you?

The Bible calls both of these things "the fear of man."

Earlier in Acts chapter 5, Ananias and Sapphira had sold some land and pretended to give all of their earnings to the church. Secretly, though, they kept some of it for themselves.

Why do you think they did this? One reason is that Ananias and Sapphira feared man more than God. After they died for lying to God the Holy Spirit, verse 11 says that great fear came upon the whole church. This kind of fear was the right kind of respectful fear for God—what we referred to in our last devotion as *reverence*.

Why did Ananias and Sapphira keep some of the money for themselves and lie about it? Partly because they wanted to impress Peter and the other religious leaders by showing how spiritual they were. They wanted Peter to like them for doing something extra special. Ananias and Sapphira valued being appreciated by people more than obeying God.

Read *Proverbs 29:25*

- Do you know what a snare is? (A snare is a trap. This verse says that the fear of man—or being afraid of others' opinions of you—is a trap, one that will lead you into sin.)
- Can you think of a time when you sinned because you feared another person's opinion?

Prayer

Our Father, we have sinned against you by caring more about what others think than what you think. We've been trapped by our sin. Please forgive us for fearing the opinions of others more than fearing you. Thank you for forgiving us, and help us to revere and respect you as we should. Amen.

WEEK 11

Acts 5:12–42

DAY 1

God has the power to do miracles

[5:12] Now many signs and wonders were regularly done among the people by the hands of the apostles. And they were all together in Solomon's Portico. [13] None of the rest dared join them, but the people held them in high esteem. [14] And more than ever believers were added to the Lord, multitudes of both men and women, [15] so that they even carried out the sick into the streets and laid them on cots and mats, that as Peter came by at least his shadow might fall on some of them. [16] The people also gathered from the towns around Jerusalem, bringing the sick and those afflicted with unclean spirits, and they were all healed.

This text speaks of "signs and wonders," but another word for these occurrences is *miracles*.

A miracle is an act of God by which he sets aside the rules of what normally happens and does something very different for the sake of his glory. Do you believe God can perform miracles? Most Christians would say they do.

God loves to perform miracles by the power of his Spirit to help people believe in him.

If someone believes in the Bible, it would be hard for that person to *not* affirm miracles, because the Bible is full of stories about them. Jesus performed many miracles while he was on this earth, and his first followers did many as well.

But do you know why God loves to perform miracles through his people from time to time? The answer might have something to do with Jesus' return, which we talked about a few weeks ago. When Jesus returns, he will fix everything that is broken; there will be no disease, death, or sin.

Jesus and his first followers performed miracles to demonstrate God's love, but also to foreshadow the perfection and justice that will be enjoyed during this coming age when Jesus returns and reigns. Miracles signal the reality that God's kingdom has been initiated on earth, reflecting his will to restore all things. Demons are cast aside, the physically broken are restored, and the scary storms are calmed.

Isn't that cool?

The purpose for miracles is partly to remind us that God is the true God, and only his power can manifest miracles. When Jesus returns, his will on earth will be completely done "as it is in heaven." Miracles remind us that this day is coming—and soon.

Read Isaiah 11:6–9

- Would you say that the events you read about in this text sound miraculous? (Yes, they're very abnormal circumstances.)
- Does this scenario sound good to you?

Prayer

Our Father, thank you that you sometimes break the rules of creation to show us your glory, power, and dominion over the earth. Thank you that you show us your love and restore that which is broken. We long for the day when this will be completely finished and we will live with you forever. Amen.

DAY 2

No stopping God's Word

[5:17] But the high priest rose up, and all who were with him (that is, the party of the Sadducees), and filled with jealousy [18] they arrested the apostles and put them in the public prison. [19] But during the night an angel of the Lord opened the prison doors and brought them out, and said, [20] "Go and stand in the temple and speak to the people all the words of this Life." [21] And when they heard this, they entered the temple at daybreak and began to teach.

God loves his Word. He loves to communicate. He loves to help people understand who he is and what he has done. Isn't that great?

If you just received the best news in the world about something, wouldn't you want to tell someone or everyone?

God is the same way. He loves to tell people the best news in the world. He did that through Jesus and his earthly ministry, and he does it through us when we read his Word and tell others about Jesus.

Did you know there are places in this world where people hate God and don't allow anyone to talk about Jesus? It's true. This means there are people who have never heard about Jesus, and that's why we need to go and share his message!

But it's not always easy. Some people who go on mission for Jesus end up in prison, just as the apostles did in Acts chapter 5. Does imprisoning God's messengers stop his plan from going forth? It never does. God will accomplish his purposes no matter what.

For that we should be very thankful.

Read *Isaiah 55:10–11*

- Can anything thwart God's purposes? (No. It will succeed.)

Prayer

Our Father, thank you for giving us your Word and promising to accomplish your purpose through it. We pray you would strengthen those who are in prison because they love Jesus. Remind them that your first followers also endured the same hardships. In spite of their circumstances, may you use them to preach your Word to all who will listen. Use us to move your Word forward in our world as well. Amen.

DAY 3

Obey God

[5:29] But Peter and the apostles answered, "We must obey God rather than men."

Most of us have probably disobeyed our parents at some point. Can you remember a time when you did?

If so, how did things turn out? You likely learned that disobedience isn't worth the price tag it comes with. Obeying your parents, on the other hand, brings honor to them as well as to God.

Hopefully this will never happen, but imagine a scenario where suddenly one day your parents insist that you forsake Jesus. In spite of what we just talked about, would this be a good time to disobey them? Sadly, it would. There are times to obey and times to disobey. If you are ever confused about how to make such a decision, it's always good to ask a trusted relative or pastor.

In our text for today, we see that Peter and the apostles are told once again to stop talking about Jesus. But they aren't swayed, for they know that obeying God is vastly more important than listening to men who don't know him at all.

Do you think they made the right choice?

For most Christians, there comes a time when one must decide which is better—obedience to men or obedience to God. When faced with that decision, we should pray to our Father in heaven and seek advice from brothers and sisters who know and love God and his Word.

Read *1 Corinthians 10:31*

- What should be our goal in any circumstance we find ourselves in? (To bring glory to God.)
- Have you ever been in a situation where you felt pressure to "fit in" instead of obeying God and giving him glory?

Prayer

Our Father, give us wisdom and strength when we find ourselves in situations that are very challenging to navigate. We are weak and need your help. We know you have promised to give it by your Spirit, and for that we are thankful. Give us eyes of faith to persevere. Amen.

DAY 4

Nothing can stop you

[5:38] "So in the present case I tell you, keep away from these men and let them alone, for if this plan or this undertaking is of man, it will fail; [39] but if it is of God, you will not be able to overthrow them. You might even be found opposing God!"

Have you heard of Michael Jordan or LeBron James, two of the best basketball players God ever created? They possess physical abilities for playing the game that no one comes close to touching.

Now imagine playing basketball in the driveway with your friends, and LeBron James shows up and asks to be on your team. Do you think the other team stands a chance? No way. LeBron would slam dunk on your friends hard enough to make them cry.

This scenario is similar to what's happening in the text we read today. The religious guys who oppose Jesus and his followers were talking about what they should do, since these followers of Jesus just wouldn't stop talking about him. One of the leaders stood up and said they should be careful; if by some chance God just happened to be on the disciples' team, then they would certainly not fare well on the opposing team. Their fate might involve something worse than getting dunked on.

So they decided to leave the disciples alone for a bit.

It's not wise to play against God's team.

Read *Romans 8:31*

- Why should we not fear when people are against us? (Because God is for us.)
- Is any force of opposition ever capable of succeeding against us? (No, because God is in us, and he is never defeated.)

Prayer

Our Father, thank you that you are with us and that nothing can stop you and your plans. We rest in that fact. Amen.

DAY 5

Rejoicing in persecution

[5:39] So they took his advice, [40] and when they had called in the apostles, they beat them and charged them not to speak in the name of Jesus, and let them go. [41] Then they left the presence of the council, rejoicing that they were counted worthy to suffer dishonor for the name. [42] And every day, in the temple and from house to house, they did not cease teaching and preaching that the Christ is Jesus.

Does something about today's passage strike you as odd? How did Jesus' first followers react after getting beat up for speaking about Jesus?

The Bible says they rejoiced! Isn't that crazy? Why would they do that?

It might have something to do with the fact they had closely followed Jesus during his earthly ministry, and Jesus himself had been severely persecuted. Jesus told them that if the world persecuted him, it would persecute his followers, too.

But why rejoice?

These believers loved Jesus so much that they wanted to prove they were his

DAILY DEVOTIONS

followers. Suffering the same opposition that Jesus faced proves they were preaching Jesus' same message. It means they were faithful! They didn't back down, and they didn't deny Jesus just because of difficulties.

Persecution will always prove who Jesus' real followers are. Many leave the faith if it gets hard. But true disciples of Jesus stay with him no matter what, and we see this illustrated in today's text.

Read *Matthew 10:16–18*

- How does God want us to act when we are persecuted? (Wise and innocent.)
- Have you ever been persecuted for your faith? If so, how did you respond?

Prayer

Our Father, thank you for the times when our faith is tested. We need your strength to endure and persevere when that happens. Give us the grace to speak without fear and to continue in the faith no matter what. We need you—please help our unbelief. Amen.

SMALL GROUP STUDY

WEEK 1

Acts 1:1–11

Read *Acts 1:1–11*

Jesus is alive! The Bible teaches this, showing it to be true on every page, and it promises he will return. Much like the apostles, we too have our own ideas about what we'd like Jesus to do for us (e.g., "Lord, will you at this time restore the kingdom to Israel?"), but Jesus graciously keeps the apostles—and us—on track. In the meantime, for those who are in Christ Jesus, God the Holy Spirit will come in power, enabling them to witness to others the powerful work of Jesus' death, burial, resurrection, and ascension.

Questions

- Do you believe Jesus Christ is alive?
- Is the Holy Spirit living inside of you?
- Who are you witnessing to about what Jesus did and taught?
- Which proofs of Jesus' resurrection mean the most to you?

Prayer

Thank you, Father God, for sending Jesus to die for our sins and save us from death. Not only did Jesus save us from death, he also saved us so we could witness about him. Please give us power through your Holy Spirit to boldly proclaim to those in our homes, neighborhoods, workplaces, schools, and cities—even to the ends of the earth—all that your son Jesus did and taught. Thank you that you are sending Jesus back in your wise timing and that, in the meantime, salvation from God has been sent to us. We pray this in Jesus' name. Amen.

WEEK 2

Acts 1:12–26

Read *Acts 1:12–26*

How do you manage to respond to the difficult issues of life? We don't often have to face outright betrayal in a small group context, as reflected in this week's reading. But we can learn from how the early believers faced the problem. We must gather as a community to pray for guidance when God is calling his people to mission.

Questions

- Does your group pray together? Are you praying for your leaders and asking God to put the right leaders in place where there are needs? What inhibits you from praying together? What encourages you to pray together?
- As leaders in the church leave, who steps up to lead? Have you been called to serve?

Prayer

Thank you, Father God, that you've called us in specific ways to serve you and your church. I ask that you'd draw us, both men and women, to one accord and prayer. Please lay a conviction on our hearts to serve your church, and provide ways for us to lead others in this way. Thank you for providing strength for the work you've called us to.

WEEK 3

Acts 2:1–13

Read *Acts 2:1–13*

This week's Scripture passage depicts the wonderful scene at Pentecost: the Spirit's presence is experienced as a rushing wind and fire. Simple fishermen begin speaking in foreign languages about the mighty works of God while onlooking crowds are confused by what they see and hear.

No doubt this is a strange scene. But even more strange are the measures people take to avoid the truth that Jesus is God and that he came to save sinners. The crowd's version of making sense of the situation here is to believe that all those preaching in their own languages are drunk! That seems like a pretty unlikely explanation. Who's heard of a party where people drank too much wine and began speaking in languages they didn't previously know? Maybe this "new wine" was pretty special.

Those who have eyes to see will realize that the striking thing about this scene is God's desire for all people of every nation and tongue to hear the good news of Jesus. God will go to great lengths—including gifting believers with the miraculous ability to speak unknown languages—so that the good news of Jesus is proclaimed to all people.

Questions

- The Holy Spirit is associated with "rushing wind" and "fire." We don't often see God working in these kinds of ways, but even when we don't, the Spirit is definitely still at work. How have you seen God the Spirit move powerfully in your life and community? How would you like to see him move? Take time to pray for this in group.
- What gifts has God given you, and how are they benefitting the church as you use them to proclaim the kingdom?
- How do you specifically need power from the Holy Spirit to do what he's called you to do? Take some time to pray for one another in group.

Prayer

Father God, thank you for sending your Spirit to fill both men and women, so they can say and do powerful things. In word and deed, you empower us so that lives are changed. Please empower us to tell of your mighty works, to the amazement of others, for the sake of your glory and our joy.

Witness

"I used to have my small group at a local bar. I didn't quite know how it would all work out, but as we gathered each week to discuss the content from the previous weeks' sermons from church, I was hoping for—and expecting—Jesus to save people who were relationally connected to the men in the group. Jesus did above and beyond what I had hoped for. I wanted to see one unbeliever meet Jesus. Instead, I saw Jesus save ten men, women, and children who were connected to the men in the group. I saw him heal marriages, and I saw him rescue those tormented by the enemy. I saw couples come together and get married. I saw him multiply one group into three, and each of those groups have continued to multiply to this day. The stories of salvation connected to these groups continue."

WEEK 4

Acts 2:14–41

Read *Acts 2:14–41*

Hundreds of years prior to the day of Pentecost, through the prophet Joel, God the Father promised to pour out his Spirit. The miraculous still occurs in our day, and some people are specifically gifted by the Spirit to see visions, dream dreams, and prophesy. But don't miss the big idea: God's plan is to use these things not as ends in themselves but as the fulfillment of prophecy and as signs pointing to Jesus. The point is that Jesus Christ saves everyone who calls upon his name. Jesus died for our sins, was raised up by God, and has freed us from death. He now rules as King at the right hand of the Father. This wonderful truth cut its listeners to the heart back then, even as it does today. How should we now respond? What should we now do? The same as then: repent and be baptized. Obey God's call. The church grew from 120 souls to 3,120 souls in one single day! To see the Spirit moving in our churches like this is something we should pray for and joyfully expect until that "great and magnificent day" when the Lord returns.

Questions

- Have you called upon the name of Jesus to be saved? If so, what is next? If not, what holds you back from him?
- Those of you who have come to Christ, have you been baptized? If not, when is the next baptism service at your church?
- Who, by name, are you praying will be added to our number?

Prayer

Father God, please save those we've been witnessing to. Please give them faith to call on the name of Jesus and be saved. Give us the right words, so we can share with them how good and powerful you are, and that you love us so much that you sacrificed your Son for us while we were still sinners (Romans 5:8). Thank you for keeping your promise to give us your Son and your Spirit. May more be added to our number daily.

Witness

"There was a young boy from the kids ministry who came to his mom. He was obviously distraught and said, 'Mom, I'm separated from God, and I don't want to be separated from him.' She asked him what separated him, and he said, 'my sin.' She called her husband over so he could join the conversation, and they talked with their son about his sin and need for a Savior. He prayed and believed in Jesus. And he's only three years old!"

WEEK 5

Acts 2:42–47

Read *Acts 2:42–47*

This Scripture passage portrays the best picture of a small group—ever. As the early church grew, they devoted themselves to the Word, prayer, and fellowship, sharing meal after meal as they gave generously and watched God do amazing things in their community. These were not religious duties they were obligated to fulfill; these were things they longed to do, things they were *privileged* to do. The early church's example paints a clear picture of what today's believers should be devoted to (i.e., the Word and prayer) and demonstrates how we can practically love and care for one another.

Questions

- This section of Acts isn't necessarily a prescription for Christian community, but it does illustrate what a Spirit-filled community values and how they care for one another.
- Does your small group resemble the early church? How would you like your group to grow in light of this week's text?
- What keeps you from experiencing community as the early church did?
- Do you have any needs that could be met by other members of the group, or do you know of others in the group who have needs you can help with?
- Have you seen someone saved by Jesus recently? Share this with your group and celebrate together.

Prayer

Father, please bless us with a warm, giving community as seen in the book of Acts. We have community with you through Jesus' sacrifice and the Spirit inside of us, but we don't always feel this with our brothers and sisters. Make our meals together sacred and joyful, and make a way for those who are far from you to join in our fellowship.

Witness

"Our small group has an unbelieving gal named Katy. She came to group in a pretty tough spot. She was friendless and without a car, and basically she was finding her community in the beds of dudes from bars. By God's grace, Katy is now growing in Christian community by attending our group. We raised money and helped her buy a car. Now she is a good friend who is completely involved in our group, and she's starting to question her identity as someone who allows guys to use her. This week she told us how blessed she feels being with us, her new friends who love her without judgment. I believe it's only a matter of time before Jesus will save her."

WEEK 6

Acts 3:1–10

Read *Acts 3:1–10*

In the Gospels we see Jesus having compassion for the sick and infirm. Through the Spirit, the early church was also given this same power and authority to heal in the name of Jesus. Jesus continues to heal the sick even today, and he does it through his people.

This text also gives us a picture of an appropriate response to Jesus's miraculous healing power. A social outcast—a beggar lame since birth—is welcomed into God's family when Jesus instantly heals him. The formerly disabled man leaps up and down for the first time, praising God with joyful worship. Not only had his physical body been healed; his eternal soul had also been saved. This man asked for one thing—money—but God surprised him abundantly above and beyond his request.

God loves to give good gifts to his people. To paraphrase C. S. Lewis, it's not that our desires are too strong, it's that they're too weak. We're like little kids in the slums who are content to make mud pies when we're offered a vacation at the ocean.[1] Have you played it safe when it comes to asking God for the desires of your heart? Why?

Questions

- We are not much different from the lame beggar. Though our experiences may not include miraculous physical healing, we all were in a state of desperate need prior to being saved by Jesus. If you have a story of healing (physical or otherwise), share it and celebrate with the group.
- Do you need prayer for healing? Have you asked your church elders to anoint you with oil (James 5:14)?
- Have you seen anyone healed before? Share with the group.
- This text gives us a clear picture of Peter's and John's intentionality with the lame man (v. 4: "Peter directed his gaze at him, as did John, and said, 'Look at us.'"). Is God calling you to this kind of focused pursuit—one where you clearly explain to someone the saving power of Jesus Christ?

---

[1] C. S. Lewis, *The Weight of Glory and Other Addresses* (Grand Rapids, MI: Eerdmans, 1965), 1–2.

Prayer

Father, we know you have the power to heal, and we know of people who need healing. Please send your Spirit to bring healing to those we lift up in prayer. As you act in miraculous ways in our community, may we be filled with awe and reverence for your power. I ask that the same wonder and amazement we experience would be felt by those who are still far off from you, and that you would draw them closer to you through your Son, Jesus.

Witness

"After suffering postpartum bleeding for nine weeks and being on bed rest for five weeks, my doctor recommended a surgical procedure that would remove the cause of the bleeding. But because I was caring for a newborn and taking care of four others kids, a surgical procedure seemed daunting and borderline impossible for our circumstances. That Sunday, our pastor invited the congregation to come up for prayers of healing. I'd never heard one of our pastors extend this particular invitation before. My husband and I had been praying about this together, but I felt compelled to accept the offer. The process was beautiful—reading through James 5 with a deacon, confessing sin, praying for ourselves and one another, then meeting with a pastor who anointed me with oil. When I was anointed, my abdomen filled with warmth, and I thought that even if the bleeding wouldn't stop, I'd be okay with it since I knew the Lord had at least physically placed his hand on me. But by the end of the day the bleeding had lightened; Monday night it was nearly gone; and by Tuesday morning it had completely stopped! Now I have a conviction to pray for healing!"

WEEK 7

Acts 3:11–26

Read *Acts 3:11–26*

It's tempting to take credit for God's work in your life, isn't it? Once Peter had the crowd's attention, he could have easily basked in glory for the heroic act of healing this man's broken body. Instead, he clearly redirected the praise and gave center stage to Jesus. What a wonderful example for us!

Peter took the opportunity offered by this miracle to address the utterly astounded people, proclaiming to them their own unrighteousness and promising that their sins would be blotted out when they came to Jesus. Yes, God's gift of healing is amazing. But even more amazing is God's graciousness to turn us from our sins (v. 26) amid our ignorance of him (v. 17) and our outright rebellion.

Questions

- Jesus was appointed for your salvation. Do you have faith in his name?
- Peter was very bold in naming sin. What sins in your life need to be named, confessed, and repented of? What would keep you from walking in the light with your small group?
- Verses 19–20 connect repentance with refreshing that comes from the presence of the Lord. In what ways have you experienced times of refreshing as you have repented?

Prayer

Father, thank you for sending the Author of life to die for us. Thank you for raising him from the dead, releasing death's hold on him and on us. Thank you for the name of Jesus and the saving faith all can have in that name. Please bring to mind the things you are calling us to repent of, and refresh us with your presence.

WEEK 8

Acts 4:1–22

Read *Acts 4:1–22*

Peter had miraculously healed the lame beggar by the name of Jesus Christ, who died and was raised from the dead, who is the sole source of salvation, the only name under heaven by which we must be saved. What sweet and encouraging words to hear from Peter. Jesus, born in Bethlehem and raised in Nazareth, lived a perfect life on this earth, doing what we could not and dying the death we should have, providing salvation for unworthy souls. But like the Sadducees, some may not share the joy we have in Christ.

Questions

- Before you heard the Word and believed, what deterred you from those who were teaching and proclaiming Jesus? If you're not yet a believer, share with the group what deters you.
- Have you ever been in a situation where you tried speaking to others about what God had put on your heart, but instead you were asked to hold your tongue? What was your response? Why did you respond the way you did?

Prayer

Father God, please enliven us to praise you when many hear the Word and believe, when we witness the sick being healed, and when opposition to the faith is overcome. We want to see you saving people in our own church and in every congregation that proclaims the name of Jesus. We ask you to fill us with the Holy Spirit, so that we're empowered to be bold. Astonish others as they see the works of God manifesting in us and through us. Thank you, Father. Amen.

Witness

Take time this week to witness to others about Jesus' saving work in your life.

WEEK 9

Acts 4:23–31

Read *Acts 4:23–31*

Group prayer time can often seem predictable. Someone requests prayer for a sick loved one, another prays for financial needs, another for guidance in dealing with a difficult teenager at home. These kinds of prayers are totally acceptable, but consider the prayer said by the apostles in this week's Scripture reading. Certainly they could have prayed for all kinds of needs. But they are about to enter into a time of persecution; they see it coming. What's striking is that they don't pray for comfort or ease, and they don't complain about their persecution. Instead, they pray for boldness in their proclamation of Jesus! They also take comfort in God's sovereignty over all things (v. 24), knowing that the opposition they face isn't outside of God's control. God answers their prayers by filling them with the Holy Spirit and empowering them to continue their mission in the face of opposition.

Questions

- Life can be complicated, difficult, and painful. Despite the scandal of Jesus' crucifixion, the believers acknowledge in prayer that all things are within God's plan and "predestined to take place." What is happening in your life right now that seems out of God's control?
- Do you ask God for boldness? If so, how does he answer your request?
- Have you faced opposition in your witness to family, coworkers, or friends? How do you need God's help in this?
- Are there people in your life with whom God is calling you to boldly share the gospel?

Prayer

Father, we ask for boldness to speak the Word of God and to be filled with the Holy Spirit. Please grant our request, and give us a sense of urgency for lost people in our lives. We praise you, Sovereign Lord, for your perfect plan that includes salvation, healing, and miracles through the name of Jesus. Thank you that because of the work of the Holy Spirit, we are never alone as we face opposition.

WEEK 10

Acts 4:32–5:11

Read *Acts 4:32–5:11*

This week's reading offers a wonderful account of the early church's unity and love. But it also presents a stark contrast reflecting the deep stain of sin—sin so serious that it results in death. All sin leads to death, but for Ananias and his wife, Sapphira, the consequence of their lies and break with unity was immediate. Imagine the hospitality team's unique task during services that week—removing two corpses from the gathering place before kids ministry lets out!

Jesus died for his bride, the church, so that its members would be one as he and the Father are one (John 17:11). In this passage from Acts, we clearly see the early believers walking out this unity in Jesus. When this couple lied and risked dismantling the unity of the church, it was no trivial matter. And it is no surprise to see the Holy Spirit responding so swiftly to protect the church in its infancy.

Questions

- How have you broken unity in the church?
- If you have broken unity, what specific steps of repentance is God calling you to?
- How do you trivialize or minimize your sin?

Prayer

Father, send your Spirit to protect our church, the bride of Jesus, from disunity. Be swift in your response, and bring people to repentance. Please continue to grow our church and allow us to have great power in giving testimony about the risen Lord Jesus. Please bring multitudes of lost men and women near to you, Father, through Jesus, by the power of the Holy Spirit.

WEEK 11

Acts 5:12–42

Read *Acts 5:12–42*

The miracles portrayed in Scripture could be called the fireworks of the Bible. And praise God for the amazing things he does in the lives of the saints! But if we're not careful, we end up missing the point of these passages. The gospel is never the side-show to miracles. Rather, in Acts, miracles accompany the forward progress of the mission of proclaiming Jesus. When God does wonderful things in and among his people, it's no surprise that Satan shows up to harass, criticize, and beat down. The fact is, the Christian life has both super-encouraging highs and deeply discouraging lows. God loves us, but Satan hates us. The more God shows his love, the more Satan spews his hatred. But remember that despite violent opposition, the same Holy Spirit who works these miracles is also empowering the church to continue in bold proclamation of the good news of Jesus.

We often cease teaching and preaching in the midst of far less opposition than the apostles ever encountered. What kind of opposition has kept you from sharing the gospel? Christians usually have no problem grasping that Jesus is their Savior. But we would do well to also remember that Jesus is King and leader, meaning his agenda for spreading the good news trumps anyone else's agenda to stop it. Certainly Christians ought to tend to their own affairs and live peaceable lives (1 Thessalonians 4:11), but there are times when God calls us to speak up and proclaim Jesus as King, regardless of the backlash.

Questions

- When you witness, do you do so in the name of Jesus?
- Have you ever suffered, in big or small ways, for being a witness to Jesus' greatness?
- What joy have you found in suffering dishonor for the name of Jesus?
- Have there been times when you ceased preaching Jesus because of opposition?
- As we speak the truth, we will face demonic opposition to the gospel. Pray for one another, that the Spirit will give strength and continued boldness.

Prayer

Father God, we are so quick to forget the power and love you have shown us, and we sometimes fail to persist in preaching the good news of Jesus when we're faced with opposition. Please forgive us for our lack of boldness and our fear of others. Please fill us with the fear of the Lord and your Holy Spirit so that we may witness "in this name"—the powerful name of Jesus.

GROUP INDUCTIVE STUDY

WEEK 1

Acts 1:1–11

Read *Acts 1:1–11*

BACKGROUND AND INTRODUCTION

In some ways, the story surrounding Jesus Christ can be difficult to believe. We seek answers to our many questions about the gospel—from Jesus' miraculous conception to his perfect sinless life. If he was God, how could he die? And if he had died, how could he rise? These questions have been asked by countless numbers of people for more than two thousand years.

Can you imagine experiencing these events in person? Hearing rumors about a man who truly believes he is God? Luke, author of the Gospel of Luke, was an educated doctor who was on a mission to find out the facts and record the truth about Jesus. With information proliferating by letter and word of mouth, the stories of these unbelievable experiences needed to be recorded and heard by God's people.

Originally, Luke's Gospel and Acts were one piece of writing; eventually, they were divided into two books at an unknown period in time. The gospel set the stage for how the life, death, and resurrection of Jesus would prepare the apostles, the people chosen by Jesus to start the early church, to spread his message to the ends of the earth.

Written in approximately AD 70, the book of Acts most distinctively consists of speeches or sermons (i.e., about one-third of the total text) and provides journey narratives of the Christian missionaries who preached the gospel under the influence of the Holy Spirit.

The book of Acts gives us a picture of evangelism, persecution, community, miracles, and conversion. It presents stories of the unbelievable and the unplanned—a true representation of the Holy Spirit's work in the lives of the apostles and in our lives today.

OBSERVATION

- What was Luke referring to in verse 1 when he said "the first book"?
- Who was this letter written to? What relationship did he have with the author?

- Read Luke 1:1–4. What was Luke's writing style? What was his intent? How does it compare with other genres in the Bible?
- What places and major events were referenced throughout Acts 1:1–11?

INTERPRETATION

As Luke introduced the book of Acts, he referenced Jesus' actions and the events that happened to him, providing a significant foundation upon which the rest of Acts is based. Before Jesus ascended to heaven, he continued preparing the apostles for the work they would do once he was gone. They had already spent years by his side witnessing his teaching and miracles, and later in the book the Holy Spirit was sent to further help them in their missionary journeys.

- How did Jesus prepare the disciples for life without him? Why would this have been so difficult for the apostles to understand?
- Read about the resurrection of Jesus in Luke 24:13–49. The truths of Jesus' resurrection and ascension are pivotal to the entire foundation of Christianity. Why is this? What are some of the "many proofs" (Acts 1:3) that demonstrated he was truly alive?
- In Acts 1:6, the apostles asked, "Lord, will you at this time restore the kingdom to Israel?" Why do you think they wanted to ask this particular question?
- After Jesus ascended into heaven, the apostles spent time "gazing into heaven" (v. 10). Luke also uses the word *worshiped* to describe their reaction in Luke 24:52. Why do you think they had this response? As they stood looking into the sky, why do you think they were questioned by the two men in white robes?

APPLICATION

Recently, a dear friend lost her husband to cancer. Crying out to God, she wanted to know and understand his plan. Why do young men die? What is God's plan when disaster strikes? All of us are seeking answers. And yet Jesus reminds us in this passage that sometimes it is not for us to know the plan, but to trust in the power of the Holy Spirit today (vv. 7–8).

Like the hurting, suffering people in our lives, we may not always know God's exact plan, but similar to the apostles, Jesus has given a directive to worship him and be comforted by the direction he has given through his Word. We may not see the end game, but we know that he is in charge, that he is good, and that he has given us everything we need through the empowering of the Holy Spirit.

- When you think about the future, what plans are you desperate to know about? Do you ask God for his plan or insist on your own?
- Instead of being faithful with what God has given us, we can look to the future for promised comfort, relief, security, and provision. In what ways has the Holy Spirit asked you to be faithful with what he's given now? What things are you overlooking or ignoring?
- God gives some people specific callings for their lives, but in general, he calls all Christians to live by the power of the Holy Spirit, regardless of their circumstances. One example from this passage is being his "witnesses" (v. 8). How can you grow as a witness to Jesus' work?
- Since Scripture tells us of Jesus' resurrection and ascension, we know he is alive today. Why is this comforting? Do you live in relationship with Jesus as if he is alive? How would that look different?
- The apostles demonstrate many questions and doubts as they process all they see and hear about Jesus and his plan to restore all things. They have ideas about what the coming kingdom should look like, but Jesus has other plans. What false kingdom are you putting your hopes in? How does that false kingdom get in the way of what Jesus is calling you to?

WEEK 2

Acts 1:12–26

Read *Acts 1:12–26*

BACKGROUND AND INTRODUCTION

Love and loyalty. Faithfulness and devotion. Treachery and betrayal. Murder and suicide. Hope, expectation, and restoration. Such are the elements permeating Luke's account of Jesus' death and resurrection and the beginning of the early church. The tension-filled drama draws us in, then reveals a new beginning. Luke's Gospel tells a real story, and it continues in Acts 1:12–26.

The early church was in its infancy, and Luke faithfully recorded the events following Jesus' ascension into heaven. Peter, the disciple who had once denied Jesus, whom Jesus exhorted to feed his sheep, now took leadership. The young church was facing a vacancy in leadership and was still reeling from the grievous recognition that one of their closest companions had betrayed Jesus. Peter pastorally guided them in understanding the circumstances and what had to take place in response. It's no accident that some of the first challenges facing the church were leadership decisions and dealing with the results of sin. God, who loves the church that Jesus died for, was preparing believers for the coming of the Holy Spirit and the future of his mission on earth.

OBSERVATION

- Where had the disciples been in verse 12? What had they witnessed while there?
- Name the men who were in the upper room in Jerusalem. What names are familiar to you? Who else was with them?
- What were the people doing in the upper room?
- How many were in the "company of persons" that Peter addressed?
- What two observations does Peter make to introduce his comments about Judas?
- How does Peter describe the story of Judas's betrayal in verses 16 and 17?
- What criteria were applied to determine who would qualify as the twelfth apostle? Who was considered?

- What two methods were employed to determine the chosen apostle? Who was chosen? Why?

INTERPRETATION

The Holy Spirit inspires Scripture, and as we study it, he reveals details that enhance and enrich our understanding of his intent. A close look at these questions helps us uncover some of the finer points of this passage that we might otherwise overlook.

- The short Sabbath-day walk that Luke recorded suggests the disciples might have stayed in an upper room not far from the temple. Review Luke 24:50–53. What were the disciples doing in verse 53? How does this complement Acts 1:14? In what two activities were the people engaged? What does this tell us about the community of believers? What were they praying for? (See Acts 1:4, 5, 8.) What can we learn from their example?
- Read Acts 1:14, 4:24, and 5:25. The early church functioned as a community, not only sharing food and possessions but also oneness of agreement and purpose. The Greek word *homothumadon* is translated "with one accord." Luke uses this word ten times, and it occurs only once elsewhere in the New Testament. What do these verses signify about the Christian community in Acts?
- Read Luke 24:25–27, 32, and 45–49. What do these verses tell us? To whom do the Scriptures point? Now read Acts 1:15–17. Peter laid the foundation for replacing Judas by pointing to the authority of Scripture. What truths do these three verses affirm about Scripture? What does this tell us about the character of God?
- Jesus taught the disciples that Old Testament Scripture confirms God's plan. Read Psalm 69:25 and Psalm 109:8 and compare these verses with Acts 1:20. What Old Testament prophecies were being fulfilled in this situation? What does this tell us about God's intentions for the church?
- Review Acts 1:21–26. Following Judas' treachery, the Twelve needed to be restored. Why? Why was it important that the specifications for an apostle were fulfilled? This is the last instance in Scripture of casting lots. Why did they cast lots? Why was the casting of lots no longer needed after this?

APPLICATION

- The early church has much to teach us about perseverance in prayer. What are you bringing before God in persevering prayer? What gives you the confidence to continue?

- How do you discover God's will? It's not likely that you cast lots! This passage shows us that the guidance of Scripture, prayer, and common sense are three reliable ways through which we can discern God's direction in our lives. Have you ever heard someone justify sinful actions by saying, "God told me. . ."? How does Scripture reveal right action to us? (See 2 Timothy 3:16.) Do you consult the wisdom of godly counselors? (See Proverbs 11:14, 27:9.) How do you pray to discern God's will?

- Judas hardened his heart in the face of God's grace. Despite walking with Jesus, witnessing miracles, and seeing God's redemptive plan unfold before his very eyes, he was complicit in Jesus' murder. Reformer John Calvin says, "Judas may not be excused on the ground that what befell him was prophesied, since he fell away not through the compulsion of the prophecy but through the wickedness of his own heart."[1] What have you hardened your heart to, and how have you resisted God's grace? How will you repent? What lies do you believe? What truths will replace these lies?

- All of the apostles named in this passage were witnesses to Jesus' ministry on earth and the amazing events of the early church. Many of them are never heard from again. Yet we believe they were faithful to the task given them. Most of us are not famous or renowned in any way. What is God calling you to be faithful to, even though it may not be remembered?

---

[1] John R. W. Stott quoting John Calvin. John R. W. Stott, *The Message of Acts* (Downers Grove, IL: InterVarsity Press, 1990), 54.

WEEK 3

Acts 2:1–13

Read *Acts 2:1–13*

BACKGROUND AND INTRODUCTION

Have you ever attended a sporting event and watched a team or an athlete make a dramatic entrance onto the field or toward the ring? The Holy Spirit made quite an entrance in the second chapter of Acts. Imagine yourself waiting in Jerusalem with the other believers, wondering to yourself, *Who is this Holy Spirit of which Jesus spoke?*

Yet in the midst of pondering these things, they knew they had to get to work and choose a new disciple to replace Judas Iscariot. As they were gathered on the day of Pentecost, a sound like a rushing wind came from heaven, and individual tongues of fire came to rest on each person. The Holy Spirit entered the scene! In Acts 1:8, Jesus had declared that the Holy Spirit would come upon them, giving them power to be his witnesses. Events of this week's Scripture passage confirmed this very promise.

Now imagine how this event would have boosted their morale. The prophesied coming of the Spirit was happening in their midst. At last this small, defeated, ragtag, down-and-out group of believers were receiving the empowering of the Holy Spirit and would have everything they'd need for the mission Jesus had called them to.

While the Holy Spirit has been present up to this point throughout Scripture, it is here at Pentecost that his presence began to be poured out in an ongoing way rather than as a limited allowance for specific moments of ministry. As the third person of the Trinity, the Holy Spirit was sent into the world to empower believers to live righteous lives and proclaim the gospel (John 14:16–17; Acts 1:1–8; Luke 24:49). He counsels and comforts believers (John 14:16; Acts 9:31). He teaches and guides believers (John 14:26; Acts 8:29). He convicts of sin and leads them toward holiness (John 16:8–11; Galatians 5:16–25). He prays on behalf of others (Romans 8:26–27).[2] And he empowers Christians to do the work they have been called to (Luke 4:18–19; 1 Corinthians 12:11). Pray that the Holy Spirit will be active in your life and that you will open your heart to his guidance.

---

[2] Wayne Grudem, *Systematic Theology* (Grand Rapids, MI: Zondervan, 2000), 232.

OBSERVATION

This section of Acts is pivotal to the rest of the book as well as the rest of the New Testament. The disciples received direction for accomplishing the mission God had laid out for them as he blessed his people with the Holy Spirit, filling them with his presence and enabling them to witness his power to others.

Read *Acts 2:1–4*

- When and where does this event take place?
- Who is there?
- What signs accompany the presence of the Holy Spirit?

Read *Acts 2:4–13*

- Where are the devout men from?
- Describe the two responses to hearing the disciples speak in other tongues.

INTERPRETATION

Some may correlate the "other tongues" spoken by the 120 believers at Pentecost to the passages on tongues in 1 Corinthians 12 and 14. But the narratives in Acts and 1 Corinthians are divergent in their expression and purpose. At Pentecost, there was no need for an interpreter because the Holy Spirit enabled the speakers to communicate in the diverse languages of the hearers. The 1 Corinthians passages, however, specify that tongues need interpretation and are largely for personal edification and enhancing one's connection with God (1 Corinthians 14:2).

- Leviticus 23:15–16 commands the Israelites to celebrate the Feast of Weeks, or Pentecost (a transliteration of the Greek word *pentikosti*, which means "fiftieth"), on the fiftieth day after Passover. Within Jewish history, this date is also known as the anniversary of the giving of the Law at Mount Sinai (Exodus 19:1). Why do you think God filled the believers with the Holy Spirit on this same day? (For further study, see Matthew 5:17–20; Luke 24:36–49; Romans 8:1–11.)
- Acts 2 has a mission-oriented thrust. In addition, it also presents a picture of the reversal of what happened in Genesis 11, where God used different languages to divide the people who are building the Tower of Babel. Acts 2 recounts these people groups and their varying languages being drawn together. Before Jesus ascended into heaven, he commissioned the disciples

to go into all the earth and make disciples of all nations (Mark 16:15; Matthew 28:19). How does the believers' sudden ability to speak in other tongues fit with these verses?

APPLICATION

There are various ways people respond to the biblical account of the giving of the Holy Spirit. Some are completely confused about the idea of a mystical spirit, while others can identify because they have felt his presence. At times, our lack of understanding regarding the role of the Spirit, and sometimes poor teaching, can lead us to believe the work of the Spirit is baffling or scary. We can be tempted to mock others' experiences or safely try to figure it out on our own. Regardless, it's clear that as the Spirit worked in Acts, he provoked a response and drew a crowd.

- Thinking back on your personal history, what is your experience with the Holy Spirit? How does your past history color your view of this passage?
- What is your gut response to this text? Share it with the group.
- When we trust in Christ for salvation, he gives the Holy Spirit to help us and bless us. (See the introduction to this week's study.) Do you trust in Jesus and his life, death, and resurrection for salvation? If not, and you would like more information, please talk to your table leader.
- In what ways have you seen the Holy Spirit work in you or in people around you?
- This section of Acts often causes debates about the miraculous gifts. While it's true that God the Holy Spirit is at work in our present time, we can still miss the point of this passage. God has been at work throughout history, drawing all people to himself and making his redemptive plan known through fulfilling the prophecy in Joel 2:28. In short, God was ushering in a new era and gifting the early church with the empowering of the Holy Spirit. First, the Spirit brought Jesus' good news to the disciples, then to 120 Jews, then to Samaritans, to Gentiles in the surrounding area, and finally to the entire world. We are a part of the continuation of the Spirit's work in the twenty-first century. How have you seen the Spirit's work evidenced in your life? In your church community? In what ways has the Holy Spirit empowered you to help advance the proclamation of the gospel?

WEEK 4

Acts 2:14–41

Read *Acts 2:14–41*

BACKGROUND AND INTRODUCTION

The apostle Peter is a great example of someone who is empowered by the Holy Spirit. Having been a coward, Peter, full of the Spirit, was transformed into a courageous man who gave some of the most memorable sermons in Acts. Peter had previously been an uneducated fisherman who internally battled his own doubt and failures (Matthew 14:22–33; 16:22–23; 26:69–75). In Acts, however, we see a new man who unflinchingly confronted a group of Jews, directly accusing them of crucifying the Son of God, their Messiah (Acts 2:36). The Holy Spirit granted Peter the words to speak powerfully yet eloquently, piercing the hearts of the hearers, so they were convinced of their need to believe in Christ and be baptized.

OBSERVATION

This section comprises Peter's response to those who had just witnessed the believers speaking in other tongues when the Holy Spirit came upon the believers gathered for Pentecost. The astonished observers asked, "What does this mean?" (Acts 2:12). Peter explained how receiving the Holy Spirit points to and proves Jesus as Lord and Christ.

Read *Acts 2:14–21*

- Where, and with whom, did Peter stand?
- Messianic passages are those that point to the coming of a Messiah. Use the cross-reference listed in your Bible to determine which Messianic passage Peter said was fulfilled through the presence of the wind, tongues of flame, and various spoken tongues that occur at Pentecost. In Acts 2:17–18, who were affected by the Spirit being poured out?
- What wonders does God perform in the last days? Some commentators have noted that Peter was not just referencing the wonders of Pentecost, but also those depicted by the Crucifixion and in the book of Revelation.
- Who will be saved when they call upon the name of the Lord?

Read Acts 2:22–36

- To whom does the presence of the Holy Spirit point?
- Whose plan was it that Jesus be crucified? Who crucified and killed Jesus?
- Who raised Jesus up from death?
- What Messianic prophecy of David did Peter connect to Christ's resurrection? See the cross-reference for Acts 2:25–28. In Acts 2:29–35, Peter made this connection real by comparing David's status to Jesus'. Where is David now? Where is Jesus now?
- What verb was used in Acts 2:17, 18, and 33 for how God sends forth his Spirit? What does this imply about who God is?
- What final Messianic psalm did Peter use to declare Jesus as Lord? See the cross-reference for Acts 2:34–35.
- Who did mighty works, signs, and wonders through Jesus? Who promised David that he would set one of his descendants on his throne? Who promised the Holy Spirit and poured out the Holy Spirit? Who has made Jesus both Lord and Christ?

Read Acts 2:37–41

- How did Peter's audience respond to his message?
- What did Peter call them to do, and what did Peter promise them?

INTERPRETATION

Peter addressed his sermon to an audience who had just witnessed the miraculous sights and sounds that occurred when the Holy Spirit was poured out on the believers gathered for Pentecost. He used this opportunity to point to Jesus as Lord and Christ because it fulfilled the promise that God would send the Holy Spirit after Jesus' resurrection. Peter focused on the fact that these miraculous signs were evidence of a good God who has a plan for his people and draws them to repentance.

- Acts 2:17–21, if compared with Joel 2:28–32, uses a few words that are slightly different. Instead of beginning the citation with "and it shall come to pass afterward," it begins with "and in the last days it shall be," thereby implying the last days had begun. Describe the actions which initiated these last days. (See Acts 2:23–24, 32–33.) The view that we are in the last days is shared by the apostles throughout the New Testament (1 Corinthians 10:11; Heb. 1:1–2; 1 Pet. 1:20; 1 John 2:18). How does living in the last days affect how we live?

- While God planned and knew that Jesus would die and be raised, Peter attested that the Jews had crucified and killed Jesus by the hands of lawless men. How does God's plan and foreknowledge work together with people's actions?
- Peter said this message is for "everyone whom the Lord our God calls to himself." Who works salvation in the believer? According to this text, what role does the believer have in his or her salvation?

APPLICATION

- In his sermon, Peter declared they are all witnesses to God raising up Jesus and fulfilling his promise to send the Holy Spirit (Acts 2:32–33). Peter also showed that through the fulfillment of these three Messianic texts, "all the house of Israel know[s] for certain that God has made [Jesus] both Lord and Christ" (v. 36). Do you know for certain that Jesus is both your Lord and Christ? If you have any questions about what this means, or how it applies to your life, please talk to your table leader. We would love to talk with you more about it.
- After his sermon, Peter continued to bear witness to Christ and implore the people to repent. Is any part of you resisting this message? How is God calling you to respond right now?
- After receiving the Holy Spirit, Peter's life was changed, and he boldly preached the gospel to all who listened. Do you share the gospel with those who will listen? If not, what prevents you from doing so? Pair up around your table and take turns sharing the Good News. Who will you share this Good News with next—a friend, coworker, or neighbor?

WEEK 5

Acts 2:42–47

Read *Acts 2:42–47*

BACKGROUND AND INTRODUCTION

In small group ministries, we meet not only for Bible study or to reflect on weekly sermons but also to come together as the people of God. The book of Acts reminds Christians of their roots as a church that gathers in "undivided devotion to prayer, to its missionary fervor, its fellowship and sharing, its mutual trust and unity."[3]

Acts 2:42–47 occurs in the shadow of Pentecost, when the Holy Spirit was poured out on those whom God called, adding three thousand believers to the church in one day. The people witnessed the love of God the Father through the grace of Jesus and experienced fellowship with one other through the Holy Spirit (2 Corinthians 13:14). This week's text shows us what the Triune God does next.

OBSERVATION

Verse 42 says the believers were "devoted to," or "steadfastly attentive to," the teaching of the apostles. They were hungry to learn about Jesus and to worship him. When the apostles, full of the Holy Spirit, preached Christ crucified, God worked with wondrous signs and miracles, and the people stood in awe of God's greatness. These believers—the church, or the unified body of Christ (Ephesians 4:4)—could not stand having plenty while their new brothers and sisters were in need, so they sold their possessions and lovingly gave to one another.

In verses 42 and 46, the "breaking of bread" may be a reference to the Lord's Supper (Communion), or it may just be a shared meal. Either way, they were experiencing life together—in large groups in the temple and in small groups in homes—by eating, worshipping, and praying together. Their fellowship flowed from a shared awe of God. Through their unity, the Holy Spirit was also drawing others and growing his church every day.

- What was the "fuel" for the believers' devotion to the apostles' teaching? Why?

---

[3] John B. Polhill, Acts, vol. 26, *The New American Commentary* (Nashville, TN: Broadman & Holman, 1992), 72.

- What response did teaching about Jesus, along with signs and wonders done through the Holy Spirit, produce in them?
- How did having great awe for God change how they treated one other?
- When the believers experienced this fellowship, what was the Holy Spirit doing to their numbers?

INTERPRETATION

The Greek word for fellowship is *koinonia*, which comes from the root word meaning "common, having in common, sharing." Acts 2:42, 44–45 describe what this fellowship looked like. We catch another glimpse in Acts 4:32–37. Here the believers spontaneously responded to specific needs among them. It was not forced. As they experienced all that God was doing, they were filled with glad and generous hearts and responded by welcoming others into their homes and sharing all they had.

- Read Colossians 3:12–17. Why do you think Paul told us to "put on" these qualities? What does love do to a community? Where does this love come from?
- This perfect fellowship did not last forever. Read Acts 4:32–5:11. Sin ruined this unity and fellowship with God and others. How do you respond to conflict in community?
- Read 1 Corinthians 10:16. *Koinonia* is translated here as breaking bread. How does taking Communion reflect fellowship with Christ and corporate identity with the body of Christ?
- In John 4:48, Jesus reprimanded an official for wanting signs and wonders. In Acts, however, the believers witnessed signs and wonders as evidence of God's work. What response did signs and wonders provoke in them? Was it sinful to base their faith on these? What else drew people to the early church?

APPLICATION

Abiding in Christ leads us to love biblical teaching, witness the Spirit's work in our lives, and live worshipfully and prayerfully with other believers. Closeness with our Savior leads us to do things we never thought possible.

- What prevents you from being hospitable? Is there something else you're more devoted to that would keep you from hospitality?
- The young church daily saw the deliverance and healing of sinners. Is this your experience? How does the busyness of life hinder seeing this?

- What "blinders" are preventing you from seeing the needs of others? How does your love for possessions keep you from loving Jesus and others?
- How is pride inhibiting your full enjoyment of Christ and your fellowship with other believers? Are you waiting for signs and wonders?
- Are you tempted to believe you need the next bigger and better thing instead of recognizing God's generous blessings in your life? Do you gratefully recognize his blessings in your life and respond by sharing them with others?

FOR FURTHER STUDY

The human body presents an incredible analogy to the unity of the church. Its parts are so intricate, and when they are working together in harmony, the body is healthy. Read Ephesians 4:1–16.

- What is the role of leaders in the church? What is the role of the saints?
- How is God calling you to use your gifts for building up the body?

WEEK 6

Acts 3:1–10

Read *Acts 3:1–10*

BACKGROUND AND INTRODUCTION

As Peter and John approached the temple gate to pray, they encountered a beggar asking for money. Peter wasn't able to meet the man's specific request, but instead he stressed the much greater value of God's healing and salvation over the value of money.

God's healing isn't just better; he also gives abundantly more than we ask for. The beggar didn't ask to be healed, since he believed he was incurable; he only thought to ask for what he needed to survive. But Peter and John's initiative demonstrate God's sovereign grace, acting through Jesus Christ, to rescue and restore those powerless to save themselves.

OBSERVATION

A multitude of miracles were performed after Pentecost, yet Luke singled out this one. Because the beggar had been lame since birth, it uniquely demonstrates the immeasurable greatness of Jesus' healing power and highlights the people's amazement at God's goodness.

- What is the big idea of this passage?
- What specifically is the lame man asking for?
- What active words catch your attention in this passage? Take time to write them down.
- What does this passage say about the authority given to Peter and John?
- How does the lame man respond to Peter and John and to God?

INTERPRETATION

Should we expect such miracles today? It may not be Pentecost, but Jesus' power is still evident in the church today. We should not be surprised if we hear reports of miracles. We serve a God who made all of creation and who raises the dead. What a mighty God we serve! Jesus' healing comes in many forms: he takes away sin, shame, brokenness, and disease; he heals marriages and restores families; and the list goes on.

- In verses 3–5, there is an exchange between Peter, John, and the lame man. Four different verbs linked with seeing were used. What were they?
- Through what name did they heal the lame man? Why is this significant?
- How do verses 9 and 10 describe the people's response to the lame man's new condition?

APPLICATION

This miracle story is similar in style and structure to many in the Gospels, particularly Jesus' healing of the paralytic in Luke 5:17–26. A dire need is identified and met in the name of Jesus, by the power of the Holy Spirit, through Peter and John.

The same power that was given to Peter and John works through us today. God invites us to be part of what he's doing by playing an active role in the lives of those who are suffering and in need of healing.

- Read James 5:13–16. What do these verses say about (1) our role in the church toward those who are suffering, and (2) how the Lord responds?
- We can't all identify with the physical needs of the lame man. But we can all relate to his feelings of helplessness. In what areas of your life do you hope for healing? Is it healing from the past? Is it physical in nature? Or perhaps you desire freedom from a deep sense of shame. Spend some time praying specific prayers with one another, bringing your requests to Jesus.
- God used Peter and John to heal the lame man. Peter showed both great boldness and genuine care in how he approached the man (Acts 3:4). You too can be an agent of grace and healing in the lives of others. Who is God calling you to love boldly today?

FOR FURTHER STUDY

Read Luke 15:17–26, as mentioned above, and write down the similarities you see between this miracle and the healing of the paralytic.

WEEK 7

Acts 3:11–26

Read *Acts 3:11–26*

BACKGROUND AND INTRODUCTION

The apostle Peter, with John next to him, had just healed a lame man who was lying in front of the temple. Immediately an astonished crowd gathered around them. Peter took this opportunity to preach and proclaim Christ and attribute the power of the healing to Jesus, not to himself. This is Peter's second recorded speech, the first being at Pentecost (Acts 2:14–36). Peter emphasized repentance and turning toward God instead of remaining in the ignorance of unbelief—the same ignorance that gave the Jewish leaders an explicit hand in putting Jesus to death.

OBSERVATION

- Read Acts 3:11–26. Circle any unfamiliar words or names. Who are these unfamiliar people? What do the unfamiliar words mean?
- Imagine the physical scene of what was taking place here. List some of the sights, sounds, and emotions.
- What tone did Peter take in his speech? What did he accuse the people of doing?
- What did he exhort the people to do as a response to what had been done against Jesus?

INTERPRETATION

As part of his appeal to the Jews, Luke made a reference here in Acts to the story of Jesus being handed over for death—a story he also wrote about in the Gospel of Luke. Read Luke 23:13–25 to see the connection here.

- How many different ways is Jesus referenced in Acts 3:11–26? Circle all of them. Why did Peter use different ways to address the same person?
- According to Peter, what would be results of repentance? How would they differ from what typically follows a guilty verdict?
- In verses 22–26, Peter referenced Old Testament prophets to further his appeal to the Jews. Why would this have made an impact on these

first-century Jews? What big idea was he was trying to help them see and understand?

- In verse 16, a distinction is made between "his name" and "faith in his name." What significance does this have?

APPLICATION

Those who witnessed the healing of the lame man saw a miracle happen right before their eyes. Yet they could not see the true power behind the miracle of Jesus Christ's life, death, and resurrection. Peter spoke strong words to help them see the power of Jesus, the depth of their sin, and the ultimate forgiveness that comes from Jesus alone.

The truth is, all of us are blind to the power of God's work at one time or another. Instead of attributing power to the Holy and Righteous One, we seek the words, affirmation, and power of people to bring about the specific kind of healing or miraculous signs we have in mind for ourselves. Like the Jews in Acts, we are often ignorant regarding the responsibility we bear for killing Jesus with our sin, and ignorant of the joy found in turning from our ways and trusting in Jesus for forgiveness.

- It is not always a sin to be astonished or surprised when something unbelievable happens in your life. However, the Jews in this passage responded in a way that proved they were not putting their faith in Jesus. Where do you turn in moments of disbelief or shock? Do you run toward God, or do you try figuring things out on your own, numbing out, or turning to others for answers?
- Have there been any people in your life who, like Peter, have spoken strong words that led you to repentance? What was that like for you? Have you been able to specifically acknowledge and thank them for allowing God to use them in this way?
- Peter showed boldness, passion, and conviction in calling the Jews to trust in Jesus and repent from their sin. He did not shy away from difficult words, but he also instilled hope through what he was calling them to. Are there people in your life God has called you to be bold with? Who can you pray for? Name those whom you are trusting Jesus to bring to repentance.

WEEK 8

Acts 4:1–22

***Read** Acts 4:1–22*

BACKGROUND AND INTRODUCTION

Earlier in Acts chapter 1, prior to his ascension to heaven, Jesus told the disciples that in just a few days they would be baptized with the Holy Spirit: "You will receive power when the Holy Spirit has come upon you, and you will be my witnesses in Jerusalem . . . and to the end of the earth" (Acts 1:8).

In Acts chapter 4, Peter and John, apostles of Jesus Christ, were taking their call very seriously. They traveled around Jerusalem, boldly healing the sick in the name of Jesus. They passionately and fearlessly preached Jesus' resurrection to very large crowds, and many were converted. How could they possibly have the courage and boldness to proclaim these things to the very same group of religious leaders who had killed Jesus only a few short weeks before? It seems they could expect to meet a similar fate. The only answer is that the promised Holy Spirit had filled them with power and courage. Even in the face of real and present danger, they received boldness from the Holy Spirit, personifying the faithful witnesses Jesus spoke of in Acts 1:8.

As followers of Jesus, faith is to the key to allowing the Holy Spirit to speak through us. This faith in itself is a gift of the Holy Spirit. The very same Spirit who empowered Peter and John to powerfully proclaim the gospel of Christ is given to followers of Jesus today. We are "baptized" in the Holy Spirit in the same way the early church was baptized, though we will likely never face the danger and adversity they experienced unless we travel to areas where believing in Jesus is a crime.

OBSERVATION

Reread Acts 4:1–22 and make a list of who is mentioned in this section of Scripture.

- Who were the main characters portrayed in Acts 4:1–22? Indicate their role if it is provided in the text.
- Which religious sect was prominent?
- Who was the high priest at the time?
- What appeared to be the main theme(s) of this text?
- What did Peter proclaim in verse 12?

Now make note of the obvious facts that are stated, such as gatherings, actions, and key statements made in the text.

INTERPRETATION

Let's shift our focus and try to understand the significance of the events noted in this section of Scripture—why the people responded as they did and what impact this had on furthering the gospel of Christ.

- Who were Peter and John speaking to when the religious leaders came upon them, and why were they speaking with this crowd?
- Why were the leaders so annoyed? What wrong did Peter and John do in the eyes of the religious leaders?
- What did this religious sect believe, as stated in the text?
- What did Peter accuse these leaders of doing?
- What action did the leaders determine to take with Peter and John, and why?

APPLICATION

- Prior to receiving the Holy Spirit, Peter was timid, even cowardly, about his faith in Jesus. In what ways have you responded out of fear, like Peter did, regarding your convictions about Jesus? When have you declined opportunities to proclaim the name of Jesus by sharing him with another person, out of a desire for your own comfort? Does knowing how the Holy Spirit faithfully empowered the apostles give you new courage to face these conversations more confidently in the future?
- How has your desire to be accepted, liked, and wanted by others influenced your witness for Jesus?
- Peter and John were common, uneducated men. Unlike the Sadducees and Pharisees, they had not been given any kind of scholarly training. They were just everyday fishermen, but what a wealth of insight and understanding they gained as they walked and served with Jesus! Surely this kind of preparation was the best they could ever receive.
- Have you ever kept silent in conversations because you felt you lacked sufficient education or Bible knowledge? Did you effectively discount the role of the Holy Spirit in these conversations by believing your contribution could not be of value? Was it difficult to believe the Spirit would give you insight, wisdom, and understanding, as promised?

- Like the rulers, elders, and priests who confronted Peter and John, we occasionally encounter those who intimidate us. Do you willingly give them that power because you are committed to our own comfort and safety, or because you have made them out to be spiritual giants in your eyes? Have you ever asked yourself, *What could I possibly contribute to this relationship?* All people, even Spirit-filled believers, are still prone to sin and need the body of Christ to faithfully yield to the Holy Spirit's direction and influence on their behalf—for their own good as well as the good of God's kingdom and the furthering of the gospel. Ask the Holy Spirit to convict your heart if you are guilty of doing this; if he does, then ask for forgiveness. Trust that the Holy Spirit will meet you in that place of fear, just as he met the apostles.

WEEK 9

Acts 4:23–31

Read *Acts 4:23–31*

BACKGROUND AND INTRODUCTION

Sometimes it can feel like the whole world is against us; unfortunately, sometimes it really is! After the Holy Spirit had come to the early church as a virtual hurricane, sweeping in thousands of new believers, the believers were faced with their first source of opposition—the Sanhedrin Jewish religious council telling Peter and John to stop speaking and teaching in the name of Jesus. The apostles, however, were compelled to continue witnessing to what they had seen and heard. With this threat looming large, Peter and John went to their friends and prayed with fervor that God would continue granting them boldness to speak in his name, with signs and wonders following. And God responded with shattering cosmic might.

This was only the beginning of persecution directed at Jesus' church; it intensified greatly in the coming decades. In spite of this, how did the book of Acts close? With a picture of Paul, late in life, serving, preaching, and teaching "with all boldness and without hindrance" (Acts 28:31)—that is, with the same boldness in the power of the Holy Spirit given to these early church followers.

OBSERVATION

- Who did Peter and John go to when they were released from the Sanhedrin's custody (v. 23)?
- What was their friends' first instinct when Peter and John told them what had happened (v. 24)?
- What specific titles are used to refer to God and Jesus in the believers' prayer (vv. 24, 26, 27, 30)?
- What psalm do the believers invoke in their prayer (vv. 25–26)?
- What do the believers ask for boldness to do (v. 29)?
- Count how many statements in the believers' prayer are about God. Then compare it to the number of petitions included in their prayer (vv. 24–30).

INTERPRETATION

Sometimes Scripture presents just the facts about what happened or what was said, with little or no explanation. Piece by piece, the attentive and earnest reader begins to see patterns that testify to an eternal, faithful God. Be exceedingly prayerful when you approach Scripture, and ask the Holy Spirit to guide your interpretation.

- Why was it so important that the believers preface this particular prayer by acknowledging God's sovereignty (v. 24)? What, if anything, would be different if they opened with another attribute—say, "loving"?
- Before the early church went to testify about Jesus, they testified to God himself about who they knew him to be and what he was like. Why was this important? Why not just start with a prayer for boldness?
- Why do you think the believers quoted David's psalm in their prayer? What is their intent in doing so (vv. 25–26)?
- "Whatever your hand and your plan had predestined to take place" (v. 28) was a mammoth phrase. What past, present, and future events were the believers including in this "whatever"?
- Were they asking for general boldness or a specific boldness (v. 29)? What is the difference?
- Why did they ask God to perform healings and "signs and wonders" (v. 30)? What did this have to do with the opposition? (See Acts 4:14, 16.) How was this different from the situation in which some of the scribes and Pharisees asked for a sign, which Jesus rebuked (Matthew 12:38–40)?
- What do you think God was communicating to the believers when he shook the room?

APPLICATION

Persecution, the need for boldness, the power of the Holy Spirit—none of these are exclusive to the early church. This astounding story in Acts is also a model for us today.

- When Peter and John went to tell their friends about this big thing that had happened, three points stand out regarding their friends' response: (1) they listen, (2) they lift their voices to God, and (3) they do so together. It's a remarkable demonstration of empathy and intercession. How can we be more empathetic when our friends come to us? What kinds of things are helpful to do? What isn't helpful? How can we do this in unity?
- On one hand, we know these early church believers demonstrated immense

faith—they prayed, and God responded mightily. On the other hand, they weren't apostles and had no special rights and privileges. How are you stepping out in faith with expectation that God will show up in big ways?

- We know cognitively that God is sovereign over the whole world, but what about practically in your life, in your own world? Can you ask God to do "whatever" he has predestined to take place in your life, your home, your job, your family? How are persecution and opposition not outside the realm of God's guiding hand?

- In verses 29 and 31, the Greek word translated "boldness," *parrhēsia*, is important and has a different meaning from its colloquial use. Specifically, it implies an easy and open forthrightness, fearless confidence, and cheerful courage—like there's nothing to hide. What impression do you think a non-Christian has when he or she hears about a "bold Christian"? How might this understanding of *parrhēsia* better inform our witness to non-Christians?

- This boldness to speak the word of Jesus isn't derived from any special position or personal aptitude; it's something given by God and is derived from his sovereignty—we stand only in his authority. In what situations have you had an opportunity to speak the Word of God boldly—i.e., plainly and openly? What enabled you to speak? What prevented you from speaking at other times? Are there aspects of your life and faith where this kind of boldness may not apply? What happens if we're never bold to speak?

WEEK 10

Acts 4:32–5:11

Read *Acts 4:32–5:11*

BACKGROUND AND INTRODUCTION

What motivates your actions? Are you generous because you should be, or because others are watching? "For the LORD sees not as man sees: man looks on the outward appearance, but the LORD looks on the heart" (1 Samuel 16:7). If we're honest, we'd have to admit we're all motivated by self-interest at one time or another. But praise God that he gives Christians an undivided heart and a new spirit (Ezekiel 11:19). As we're empowered by the Holy Spirit, we can serve others for God's glory.

As the Holy Spirit filled the early believers, he unified them in heart, mind, and deed. They demonstrated radical generosity with their belongings, and Barnabas is introduced as a model of Spirit-filled generosity. But just as Satan entered the Garden to tempt Adam and Eve, he entered the early church through the duplicity of Ananias and Sapphira. God's response to this sin is shocking, but he will not tolerate anything that threatens to tear down Christ's bride, the church.

The Holy Spirit used the resulting fear of the Lord, along with more signs and wonders, to add even more believers to the church. People from surrounding cities gathered in Jerusalem and were changed by the gospel, and like a river overflowing its banks, Jesus' name and glory would soon spill over the walls of Jerusalem into Judea and Samaria (Acts 1:8).

OBSERVATION

As Peter and John defended the faith and the believers prayed for boldness, Luke wrote specifically about how the community was unified in everyday life.

Read Acts 4:32–37

- In Acts 4:32–33, what four descriptions are used for the community of believers?
- What were the apostles doing, and how were they doing it (v. 33)?
- How were the needs of the community being met (vv. 34–35)?

Read *Acts 5:1–11*

- Who are the characters in this section, both physical and spiritual?
- Specifically, what wrong actions did Ananias and Sapphira commit? What sin did Peter expose?
- How is the Holy Spirit at work within the accounts described in this passage (vv. 3, 5, 10–11)?

INTERPRETATION

- Unity appealed to ancient Greek sensibilities. The Pythagoreans and Plato championed no private ownership, and Aristotle wrote of a friend as "one soul dwelling in two bodies."[4] This depth of unity is apparent in the early church. How do they display the fruit of Jesus' high priestly prayer (John 17)?
- In Acts 4:36, we are introduced to Barnabas, who will later play a major role as the Acts narrative unfolds. How was Barnabas described, and why was it important at this point in the story of the early church?
- In Acts 5:3, Peter described the impetus for Ananias' actions. What specific words were used to describe Satan's entry into the narrative? Similar words were used to describe both the origin of Judas' betrayal (Luke 22:3) and the result of the believers' bold prayer (Acts 4:31). How do these three references inform you about Satan's strategy both then and now?
- In Acts 4:35, 4:37, and 5:2, we see the repetition of what phrase? What does this description mean, both literally and figuratively? Why does Luke emphasize this phrase? Ananias and Sapphira withheld money, and because of their deception, where did their lives end (Acts 5:5, 10)?
- Peter described the sins of Ananias and Sapphira in Acts 5:3 and 5:9, respectively. How did their sins differ?
- There are several important concepts mentioned for the first time in this passage. Who did Peter say Ananias lied to, and what does this tell us about the Holy Spirit (Acts 5:3–4)?
- How were the growing numbers of believers described in Acts 5:11, and in what context?

---

4 Ibid., 152.

APPLICATION

- Barnabas is offered as an example of a person who displays deep generosity. Are generous people encouraging to you? Or do you compare yourself to them in order to stroke your ego, defend your actions, enforce your brokenness, or all of the above? Is God calling you to repent of comparing yourself to other believers?
- What keeps you from giving financially in such a way that there is "not a needy person" among those in your church? How can you make practical changes so you can be even more generous? In what ways are you resisting the Holy Spirit's call to generosity?
- In some ways, we are all an Ananias or Sapphira because we say one thing but think or do another. How are you faking it with other Christians? How are you faking it with Jesus?
- Just as in the early church, God longs for unity among contemporary Christians, both within individual churches and across churches. What can you do to help unify your church? Do you need to repent of anything you may be doing that promotes disunity in the church?

WEEK 11

Acts 5:12–42

Read *Acts 5:12–42*

BACKGROUND AND INTRODUCTION

According to the World Watch List (www.WorldWatchList.us), there are twenty-three countries in the world today where Christians experience "severe" to "extreme" persecution. Most of us in the western world have never experienced opposition of this magnitude, but being challenged for speaking the truth of the gospel is hardly uncommon, even for those of us who enjoy laws protecting our religious freedom. Whether it's workplace policies that prohibit talk of Jesus, ridicule from friends and family for expressing our faith, or opposition to church involvement in local affairs, Christians are still often asked to remain silent when it comes to sharing the gospel of grace through faith in Jesus.

Up to this point in the book of Acts, life has been fairly peaceful for the early church. They were filled with the Holy Spirit at Pentecost, enabling them to spontaneously communicate with people from other nations. They witnessed supernatural healing of all the sick who were brought to their community. The church was growing in leaps and bounds with new believers being added every day. Other than Peter and John's brief imprisonment and the subsequent warning to stop spreading the gospel, we have no indication that any physical opposition to their teaching had yet come. Miracle after miracle continued to characterize the apostles' ministry.

Imagine seeing these amazing signs and wonders day in and day out . . . but suddenly something changes. The apostles were introduced to persecution at the hands of the religious and political leaders (i.e., the high priest and the Sadducees) for publicly preaching the gospel. It's really no surprise that when God moves powerfully, Satan was there to oppose the church at every turn, using whatever means necessary to bring discouragement. The apostles were imprisoned; when that didn't hold them back, they were again retained, and this time beaten. But their firm belief in the message of Jesus' death, burial, and resurrection for the forgiveness of sins was stronger than their desire for physical comfort and safety. Even in the face of difficulty, the apostles pressed on, through the power of the Spirit, and continued speaking boldly.

OBSERVATION

Read this week's Scripture passage and make some observations about the apostles' message, the resistance it received, and how they were ultimately undeterred.

- What message were the apostles teaching?
- Why were the high priest and Sadducees so opposed to their message? Where were the apostles teaching, and why was this a threat to the council?
- For what purpose did the angel of the Lord release the apostles from jail?
- What kept the apostles from being killed, thus enabling them to continue teaching about Jesus? Why was this an unlikely way for them to be spared from death? (Read Matthew 12:1–13 and John 18:1–12.)

INTERPRETATION

From the beginning of time, God had a plan for the salvation of his people. While we can glean much from this section on its own, it is really part of a greater story—one that started long before the apostles arrived on the scene, and one that involves us today.

- Read Psalm 65 and Isaiah 46:6. What has God's plan been for his people, both Jews and Gentiles, all along?
- Read Acts 1:8. According to this verse, for what purpose was the power of the Spirit given?
- What does this week's passage tell us about God's dedication to this plan? In what ways do you see the Holy Spirit actively working to ensure that the gospel was preached?
- What assurance does this give us for our ministries today?
- According to the *ESV Study Bible*, the beating described in verse 40 would have likely included up to thirty-nine lashings, with a whip made of calf's hide, on each of the apostles' bare backs and chests. Why do you think the apostles walked away from being scourged like this, "rejoicing that they were counted worthy to suffer dishonor for the name"?

APPLICATION

Like the apostles, we too have the privilege of participating in God's plan to expand his church through proclamation of the gospel. And while it's unlikely that most of us will experience the severe opposition the apostles did, we still expect to face resistance.

- The same Holy Spirit who worked miracles through the apostles (vv. 12–16) is the same Spirit who empowers Jesus' mission of bold gospel proclamation (Acts 1:8). How can you specifically ask the Holy Spirit to come upon you so you are the kind of witness Jesus is calling you to be?
- Have you experienced hostility of any kind toward your belief in the gospel? How does your own salvation and conviction that Jesus is "exalted . . . at [God's] right hand as Leader and Savior, to give repentance to Israel and forgiveness of sins" (Acts 5:31) give you confidence to press on?
- In what ways have you been fearful of sharing the gospel? Does the knowledge that the Holy Spirit actively works to bring salvation to God's people affect this?
- In what ways do you relate or not relate to the apostles' rejoicing in the face of resistance?
- When the church is on mission and the gospel is proclaimed, the church *will* experience difficulty. Our enemy is like a roaring lion looking for someone to devour (1 Peter 5:8). Have you experienced opposition to the gospel? Personal difficulty or trials? Be mindful of the schemes of the enemy, and take time to pray for strength and endurance for one another.

APPENDIX
FOR
LEADERS

APPENDIX FOR LEADERS

HOW TO USE THE DAILY DEVOTIONS

The following devotions were written in the hope that families will rally around the Word of God, grow in relationship together, and discover how the Holy Spirit fills believers, empowering them to proclaim the good news of Jesus to friends, family, and neighbors.

Every day you and your family are provided with a short passage from the book of Acts to read and discuss. A series of questions and illustrations will help you dig deeper into the passage and apply its message to your lives. Each devotion is capped off with a suggested prayer.

Don't feel bound to follow every step, read each word, discuss all the questions, or pray every prayer. Follow the Holy Spirit's lead and allow the conversation to progress as you see fit.

Also, don't stress if you miss a night or get off track with your conversation. Family time can often be a little chaotic, and things come up. Just be prepared to pick up where you left off. Most families aren't able to do devotions every night of the week, so each Scripture portion is divided into five devotions for five days of the week, allowing you the freedom to figure out what weekly rhythms make sense for you.

Finally, while the book of Acts is certainly religious history, it's also much more. Remember, God's people still have the same Holy Spirit enabling them to live with passion and partner with him to see lives changed by Jesus. That same Holy Spirit will help you and your family be bold in your witness of Jesus to one another, your church, and all those whom God has placed in your life.

HOW TO USE THE SMALL GROUP STUDY

This study has been designed to help your small group discover the power of the Holy Spirit that enables his people to provide witness to the greatness of Jesus Christ. We all need the presence of a community to encourage us when inevitable opposition to the gospel arises, and also to spur one another on to good works (Hebrews 10:24).

Each study begins with an introduction that serves as a springboard for conversation in your group. There's no need to read the introduction verbatim, if that feels stodgy. Just familiarize yourself with the content beforehand and give an overview of the Scripture passage, linking it with timely examples or testimonies of what God is up to in your own community.

After setting the stage for the week's Scripture reading, questions are provided so that the group can dive into application. Use these as a way to stir up conversation. Some questions are simply opportunities to share testimonies, while others are offered as challenges for growth. Take some time beforehand to jot down notes of what questions are best suited for your specific group, and see where the Holy Spirit leads the conversation.

Last is a suggested prayer. It's common to leave little time for prayer, but be encouraged to provide a good amount of time for this. From prayers of praise to requests for help with life's common struggles to a petition for healing, and everything in between, we need to be refreshed by God's presence and strength. Pray with expectation that God will do great things in your community. He is a loving Father who loves to give good gifts to his children.

HOW TO USE THE GROUP INDUCTIVE STUDY

What is an inductive study?

Inductive study simply means using the Bible as the primary tool for learning about God and receiving instruction about how to live a godly life. Our goals for this type of study are to observe the text, interpret its message as we listen to the Holy Spirit, and apply its meaning to our lives.

The steps are simple. Begin by reading the "Background and Introduction" of the assigned Scripture. Then read the passage and pray about what it is communicating, asking God to open your hearts and minds so that you can learn more about him.

Next, examine the passage in light of the context in which it was written, with an eye on the whole of Scripture. Then zero in on the words on the page. Good questions to ask as you study include *who, what, where, when, why,* and *how.* Here are some examples of how you might use these kinds of questions:

- Who is the writer's original audience?
- What issue is addressed? What is being said?
- Where and when did this take place?
- Why is the message given?
- How is the message communicated?

Other helpful questions are listed under the "Observation" heading.

The "Interpretation" will come from the text that is before us, as guided by the Holy Spirit, who opens our eyes and reveals what we need to see. Again, please pray that God will be guiding your mind as you examine the text. Keep in mind that as we study Acts, it's important to follow the text and let it define the context and audience before jumping into our own life application. That's where the above-mentioned questions are so helpful. Who comprised the early church as recorded in Acts? What struggles and hardships did they face? What facet of the Good News is highlighted in Acts, and why? The historical account in Acts is an exciting time in the early church. But remember, the Holy Spirit who was at work in the early church is the same Holy Spirit at work in the church today. How is the Spirit empowering the ministry you've been called to?

Next, don't miss the "Application" questions. In the fourth section of the weekly study, questions that focus on gospel application are provided. What is your plan for change, and in what ways do you need Jesus? Until the church sees how Bible knowledge relates to their own relationship with Jesus, strategies for redemption, and gospel application, it's just interesting data. Heart transformation and bold proclamation of the gospel is the goal, as the Spirit meets us in our twenty-first-century lives.

Finally, pay attention to how God is stirring and convicting your heart. It's here, at this intersection, where we apply the Word to our lives. We become more like Christ, and our relationship with God is deepened.